Egypt
Kush
Aksum

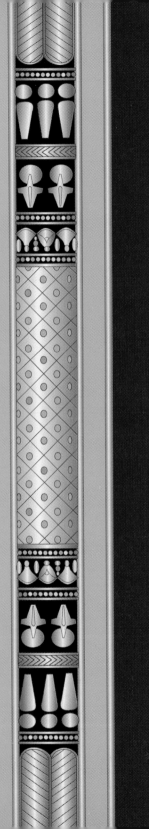

To all those whose love of history has
helped others to learn about the past and
to hope for the future.

African Kingdoms of the Past

Egypt
Kush
Aksum

•

Northeast Africa

Kenny Mann

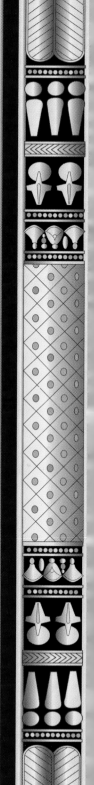

Dillon Press • Parsippany, New Jersey

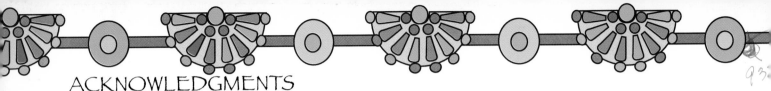

ACKNOWLEDGMENTS

The author wishes to acknowledge the interest, patience, and expertise of the following consultants: Clarence G. Seckel, Jr., Curriculum Coordinator of Social Studies, School District 189, East St. Louis, IL; and Edna J. Whitfield, Social Studies Supervisor (retired), St. Louis Public Schools, St. Louis, MO.

CREDITS

Design and Illustration: MaryAnn Zanconato
Picture Research: Kenny Mann and Valerie Vogel

PHOTO CREDITS

Front Cover: Museum Expedition, Museum of Fine Arts, Boston.
Agyptisches Museum/Universitat Leipzig: 51. Ashmolean Museum, Oxford: 62. Black Star/Griff Davis: 88. © The British Library: 84. Copyright, The British Museum: 27, 33, 54–55, 70. © Peter Clayton: 16, 19, 31, 43. Egyptian Museum, Cairo: 32. Robert Estall Photo Library/Carol Beckwith/Angelo Fisher: 76, 81, 83, 86, 95. Mary Evans Picture Library: 98. Enrico Ferorelli: 36, 44, 45, 46–47, 60–61. Graham Harrison: title page, 22. © Dave Houser: 93. Hulton Deutsch Collection Limited: 96–97. The Metropolitan Museum of Art, Rogers Fund and Contribution from Edward S. Harkness, 1929 (29.3.2): 15. Courtesy, Museum of Fine Arts, Boston: 57; Harvard University-Museum of Fine Arts Egyptian Expedition: 63. © National Geographic Society Image Collection/Georg Gerster: 10. © Dr. Paul T. Nicholson: 29, 30. © Richard Nowitz: 92. Courtesy, the Petrie Museum of Egyptian Archeology, University College, London (UC.14210): 53. © John Ross: 24–25. Topham Picturepoint: 73. © The Visitors of the Ashmolean Museum, Oxford, 1895.990/Photo by Heini Schneebeli, London: 28. Maps: Ortelius Design: 6, 18, 69.

Library of Congress Cataloging-in-Publishing Data

Mann, Kenny.

Egypt, Kush, Aksum : northeast Africa / Kenny Mann. — 1st ed.

p. cm — (African kingdoms of the past)

Includes bibliographical references (p.   ) and index.

ISBN 0-382-39657-X (pbk.). — ISBN 0-87518-655-6 (JLSB)

1. Egypt—History—To 332 B.C.—Juvenile literature. 2. Nubia—History—Juvenile literature. 3. Aksum (Ethiopia)—History—Juvenile literature. [1. Egypt—History—To 332 B.C. 2. Nubia—History. 3. Aksum (Ethiopia)—History.] I. Title. II. Series.

DT83.M317   1997

932—dc20   96-16440

Summary: This study of the traditions and history of the ancient African kingdoms of Egypt, Kush, and Aksum, which once occupied northeastern Africa, examines the kingdoms' relationships with each other as well as foreign influence and involvement in the region.

Published by Dillon Press,
A Division of Simon & Schuster,
299 Jefferson Road, Parsippany, New Jersey 07054

First edition
Printed in the United States of America
10 9 8 7 6 5 4 3 2 1

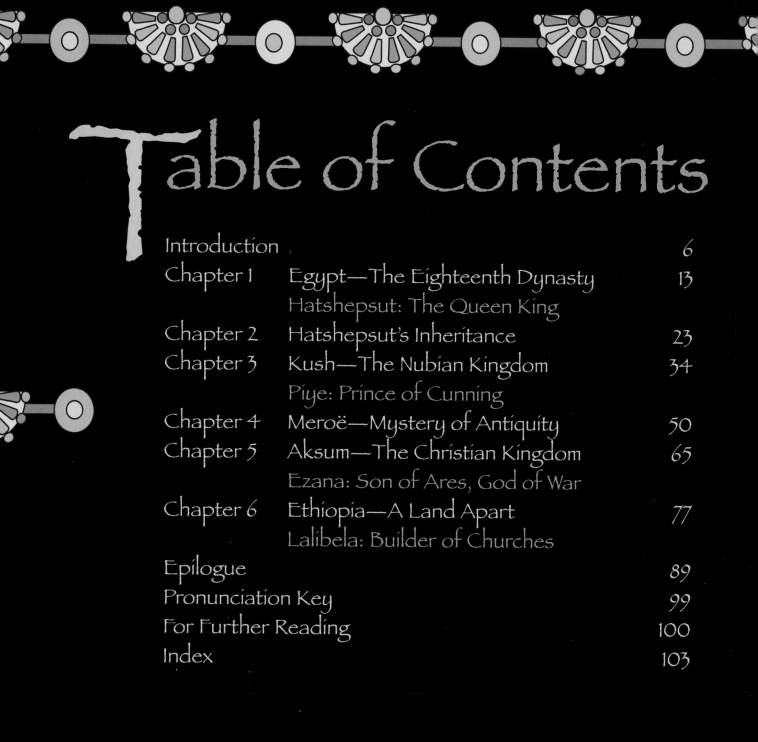

Table of Contents

Introduction 6

Chapter 1   Egypt—The Eighteenth Dynasty   13
             Hatshepsut: The Queen King

Chapter 2   Hatshepsut's Inheritance   23

Chapter 3   Kush—The Nubian Kingdom   34
             Piye: Prince of Cunning

Chapter 4   Meroë—Mystery of Antiquity   50

Chapter 5   Aksum—The Christian Kingdom   65
             Ezana: Son of Ares, God of War

Chapter 6   Ethiopia—A Land Apart   77
             Lalibela: Builder of Churches

Epilogue   89

Pronunciation Key   99

For Further Reading   100

Index   103

African Kingdoms

Note: Dates marked with an * are approximate.

10,000	**800** B.C.	A.D. **400**	**1000**

*10,000 B.C. Earliest cultivation of grains along the Nile	***700s–600s** Sabaeans emigrate from southern Arabia to Red Sea coast of Ethiopia	***A.D. 320–350** Ezana, first king of Aksum, rules
*5000–4000 Earliest permanent settlements along the Nile	**747–716** Piye rules Kush and Egypt	**327** Ezana converted to Christianity by Frumentius
*3800 Possible founding in Nubia of earliest known monarchy	**727–720** Tefnakht rules Lower Egypt	***550–1500** Christian period in Nubia
*3500–2800 A-Group in Lower Nubia	**716–702** Shabaka rules Kush and Egypt	**600s** Aksum in decline
*3500 Formation of kingdoms of Upper Egypt and Lower Egypt	**690–665** Taharka rules Kush and Egypt	**622** First year of Muslim calendar, marking Mohammed's flight from Mecca to Medina
*3100 Menes (or Narmer) unites Upper Egypt and Lower Egypt	**593** Egyptians attack Nubia and capture Napata; end of Nubian domination of Egypt	**632** Mohammed dies
2300–1500 C-Group culture in Nubia	**525** Persians conquer Egypt	**642** Roman government in Egypt overthrown by Muslims
1750–*1550 Kerma culture flourishes in Nubia	***430** Herodotus writes about Egypt	**1137** Zagwe dynasty succeeds Aksumite dynasty
1570–1293 Eighteenth dynasty rules Egypt	**300–A.D. 350** Meroitic period in Nubia	***1200–1250** Lalibela rules Ethiopia
1504–1450 Thutmose III rules Egypt	**332** Alexander the Great conquers Egypt	**1270** Zagwe dynasty overthrown by Solomonid dynasty
1498–1483 Queen Hatshepsut rules with Thutmose III	**328–308** Reign of King Nastasen in Meroë; distinctive Meroitic culture begins to develop	**1314** First Ethiopian chronicle written for King Amda Seyou
*1483 Hatshepsut dies	***323–282** Life span of the Greek priest Manetho, who arranged ancient Egypt's pharaohs into 30 dynasties	**1317** Funj sultanate established in Upper Nubia
1000 Legendary union of King Solomon and Queen Makeda		
*1000–850 Nubia disappears from recorded history	**30 B.C.** Romans conquer Egypt	

1500	**1800**	**1900**	**2000**

1500 –
present — Islamic period in Nubia

1520–1526 — Father Francisco Alvarez establishes Portuguese mission in Ethiopia

1526 — Ahmad ibn Ibrahim, known as "Gran," leads Muslim state of Adal in Ethiopia

1543 — Ahmad defeated by Ethiopian and Portuguese army

1548 — Ethiopian scholars in Rome write New Testament in Ge'ez

1684 — Job Ludolphus writes *A New History of Ethiopia*

1768–1771 — James Bruce explores Ethiopia and the Blue Nile

1798 — Emperor Napoleon of France invades Egypt

1799 — The Rosetta Stone found, providing clues to deciphering Egyptian hieroglyphics

1801 — Mohammed Ali forces French withdrawal from Egypt and takes over leadership of Egypt

1869 — Suez Canal opens

1881 — The Mahdi declares a *jihad* in the Sudan

1882 — British army occupies Egypt

1887 — Italians take northern Ethiopian province of Eritrea

1896 — Italians are defeated by Menelik II at battle of Adwa

1898 — British and Egyptians defeat Mahdist Sudanese at battle of Omduran

1914 — British declare Egypt a protectorate

1914–1918 — World War I; European powers involve their African colonies in the war

1922 — Egypt gains independence from Great Britain and becomes a democratic socialist republic

1930 — Ras Tafari becomes emperor of Ethiopia and takes the name Haile Selassie

1939–1945 — World War II; European colonies in Africa involved in the war

1941 — Italian colony of Eritrea comes under British occupation

1952 — Ethiopia regains Eritrea

1956 — The Sudan gains independence from Great Britain; Egypt gains control of the Suez Canal

1963 — African heads of state meet in Addis Ababa to form the Organization of African Unity to promote political and economic cooperation among African nations

1970 — Anwar el-Sadat becomes president of Egypt; Aswan High Dam completed

1974 — Emperor Haile Selassie of Ethiopia deposed by Lieutenant Colonel Mengistu Haile-Mariam, who introduces socialist government

1981 — Sadat assassinated; Hosni Mubarak succeeds Sadat

1993 — Eritrea becomes independent from Ethiopia

1994 — Lieutenant General Omar Hassan Ahmad al-Bashin takes over the Sudan in a military dictatorship

1995 — Ethiopia becomes a democratic federation of several regions, ruled by Prime Minister Meles Zenawi

Introduction

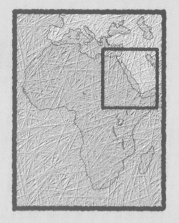

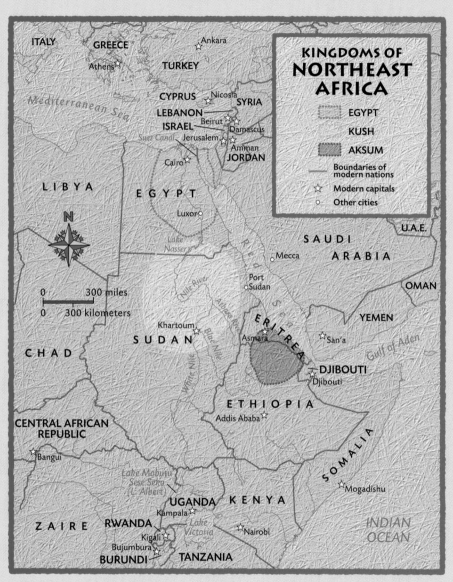

KINGDOMS OF NORTHEAST AFRICA

- EGYPT
- KUSH
- AKSUM
- —— Boundaries of modern nations
- ☆ Modern capitals
- ○ Other cities

"The names of all the gods have been known in Egypt from the beginning of time."

Thus wrote the Greek historian Herodotus, who traveled to ancient Egypt in the fifth century B.C. He marveled at the extraordinary culture he found there, and he described in detail all that he saw and learned. At this time, Egypt was a kingdom only about 1,000 km (600 mi) long and 11 km (7 mi) wide and by then was already in decline. But Herodotus recognized that Egypt was the mother of Greek civilization. He also recognized that the mother of Egypt was the Nile River.

The Nile is the longest river in the world, flowing for 6,671 km (4,145 mi) northward from the heart of Africa to the Mediterranean Sea. To the east and west of the river are harsh, waterless deserts. Agriculture is restricted to the Nile Valley, which is only a few meters wide in some places and broadens in others to a width of several kilometers. Far to the south lie the myriad swamps, tributaries, and lakes that form the Nile basin—the source of the mighty river's flowing waters.

In ancient times, people living along the Nile depended on the annual flooding of the river for their survival. Each year, starting in June, the rainy season in the far-off mountains of Ethiopia brought tons of muddy silt and surging waters down the Blue Nile and the Atbara River into the Nile, causing it to overflow its banks. The flooding usually lasted for three or four months, sometimes longer. When the waters began to recede, the extremely fertile silt was deposited on the banks of the river. Seeds could be planted on the riverbanks, and, in some areas, with careful irrigation, two crops could be harvested before

"Concerning Egypt, I will now speak at length," wrote the Greek historian Herodotus in the fifth century B.C., "because nowhere are there so many marvelous things, nor in the whole world beside are there to be seen so many things of unspeakable greatness."

The Egyptians worshiped the god Thoth, the inventor of the mathematical art of surveying. They carefully measured and recorded the rich lands flooded by the Nile each year so that property boundaries could be properly defined. Farmers paid taxes on what their land and livestock could produce, which was assessed in advance.

the next flood season. When the rains failed thousands of kilometers to the south, however, the Nile peoples to the north suffered severe famine. And when the rains were too heavy, the river could turn into a raging torrent, sweeping before it villages, livestock, and crops.

Despite such hardships, however, the Nile provided the people living along its banks with fertile soils for crops, and with water for irrigation. The river also supplied fish, hippopotamus, and other river creatures for food and was a means of transportation to distant places. Its muddy floodplains provided clay for pots and building bricks. Because they were dependent on this one resource, people living along the Nile were forced to cooperate with one another in order to make the best use of the river. Officials developed laws and oversaw land and water use. Farmers had to pay taxes to support the bureaucracy. At the head of the bureaucracy was a king, who received the taxes and used them to finance the monarchy and military, religious, and other state offices. In this way, the earliest Nile states arose around a

The ancient Egyptians called the rich, fertile valley along the Nile *kmet*, or "black land," because of the black silt deposited there. The harsh desert was called *dsrt*, or "red land."

The Great Pyramid at Giza was built by 100,000 laborers, who worked on the structure for 20 years. More than 2 million stones, each weighing 2 tons, were used in the pyramid's construction.

Very early in Egyptian history the term *per-aa*, or "great house," was coined. It referred to the royal court, or the state itself. The Greeks later translated the word as *pharaoh*, which came to mean "king."

central authority and later expanded into kingdoms or empires.

The complex geography of the river formed natural divisions between the peoples who lived along its banks. Egypt was divided into the very fertile delta region to the north, known as Lower Egypt, and the arid desert area south to Aswan, known as Upper Egypt. From its mouth to Aswan, a distance of almost 1,000 km (600 mi), the Nile is navigable. But just south of Aswan begins the first of a series of six cataracts. In these cataract zones, like the "Batn el Hajar" or "Belly of the Rocks" near the second cataract, the river plunges through stony faults and fissures and into labyrinths of deep gorges and rocky islands. Continuous passage by boat is extremely difficult and often impossible.

Between Aswan and the Second Cataract lies Lower Nubia, now part of present-day Egypt. Upper Nubia, now part of the northern Sudan, extends from the Second Cataract south to the Sixth Cataract and includes the Nile's "Big Bend." In ancient times, Nubia was known as the kingdom of Kush.

At the Sudanese city of Khartoum, the Blue Nile, emerging from Ethiopia's Lake Tana, flows into the White Nile, bringing with it about 70 percent of the Nile's waters. The Nile south of Khartoum is navigable for almost 1,600 km (1,000 mi), up to the treacherous region known as the Sudd—a vast, swampy marsh. Here, various tributaries flow into the great river. The main stream—known as Bahr al-Jebal (bahr ahl-JEB ahl)*—finds its sources in Lakes Victoria and Albert and the Ruvironza River in Burundi.

The ancient Egyptians and Nubians built not only their towns and villages along the Nile, but also their royal tombs and temples and their great pyramids, obelisks, and colossal statues. The sweat of the peasants, who labored in the nonflood season, raised these extraordinary structures. They are evidence of the ancient Egyptians' attempts to communicate with the gods and to provide for the afterlife. The sacred writings, or hieroglyphics, and pictures that appear on these stone monuments were left behind by pharaohs (FER ohz) and wealthy individuals who wished to be remembered forever, and so carved their deeds in

*Words that may be difficult to pronounce have been spelled phonetically in parentheses. A pronunciation key appears on page 99.

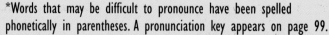

stone. These documents tell of royal births and deaths, of coronations, marriages, and religious festivals, of love between man and woman, of fishing and hunting, of war and peace.

One of the largest and most beautiful of the monuments along the Nile is the funerary temple of Hatshepsut (haht SHEP sut), one of Egypt's greatest queens. Hatshepsut's splendid monument is located on the west bank of the Nile, opposite the ancient city of Thebes (theebz), just north of the present-day town of Luxor. The steep desert cliffs here are scattered with other tombs and temples. Behind the cliffs, many pharaohs were buried in great splendor in the Valley of the Kings and the Valley of the Queens. Just as

The Egyptians believed that numbers had magical qualities and cosmic meaning. The mathematician R. A. Schwaller has suggested that their huge monuments, tombs, and temples were mathematically designed to put the Egyptians in touch with the gods.

1 — The watery abyss, called the Nun, from which creation proceeds

2 — The polarity of opposites: male/female, good/evil, positive/negative

3 — The number of relationships, expressed in triads and trinities of gods and their offspring

4 — The number of matter, symbolized by the square

5 — The number of potentiality, or eternity, expressed in the five-point star

6 — The number associated with time and space: banks of 6, 12, or 24 columns or pillars, seen at many ancient sites, symbolize the hours of the day and night

7 — The number of growth

8 — The number of sex, death, and renewal

9 — The number of pattern

10 — A return to the number one, or to the source

everyday life goes on in Luxor, so these relics across the river form an eternal companion city of the dead.

The ancient Egyptians believed that as long as images of themselves survived, and they were provided with food, clothing, furniture, servants, and everything else that had made life on earth pleasant, they would continue to live in the hereafter forever. Although she ruled over 3,000 years ago, Hatshepsut's presence can still be felt in the quiet shadows of her temple. Images of Hatshepsut show a proud and dignified face, an iron-willed bearing. Reading "between the lines" of the inscriptions that record Hatshepsut's story, one catches a glimpse of a life that

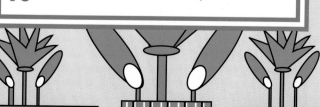

In 1956 the Egyptian and Sudanese governments decided to raise the dam at Aswan. They hoped to regulate irrigation by reducing dependency on the annual Nile floods and to provide hydro-electric power. The artificial Lake Nasser formed behind the dam threatened to submerge hundreds of Nubian monuments and temples. In 1960, UNESCO launched an international campaign to save the ancient sites. Many nations responded, sending experts and a total of almost $30 million in funds. Extensive archaeological excavations unearthed hundreds of artifacts, and most of the monuments in the region were moved to new sites on higher land. Here, crane workers help to move the head of Rameses II from his monument at Abu Simbel to higher ground. The people of Lower Nubia were forced to leave their homelands and resettle in new villages farther north. Before leaving, many kissed the graves of their ancestors. Others filled their pockets with earth—their own memento of lands that were once theirs. ▶

was full of power struggles, political intrigue, and secrets.

For most of its history, Egypt dominated Nubia. Egyptian monuments such as the huge carvings of Rameses II at Abu Simbel were intended to symbolize Egyptian power over their southern neighbor. The incredible size of these monuments and the information they provide have helped to identify ancient Egypt as one of the greatest civilizations of the ancient world. Nubia, on the other hand, had long been regarded as little more than a geographical "corridor" along which goods passed between the African interior and the Mediterranean. In the 1960s, however, the Aswan High Dam project prompted intense research into the little-known history of ancient Nubia, or Kush as it was called. Exciting findings put Nubian civilization in the limelight. Today, historians believe that ancient Nubia, or Kush, may have been founded about 3800 B.C.—some seven centuries before Egypt—and this may be the earliest known monarchy in human history.

Nubian monuments are often not as spectacular as those built by Egyptians. But research shows that the Nubian, or Kushite, civilization was, in many ways, more open to change and progress than the Egyptian. For a brief period, in the eighth century B.C., the Nubians even overcame Egypt and included it in their empire. The Nubian leader Piye (PEE ye), king of Kush, tells the story of his conquest of Egypt in detail in his famous "victory stele" (steel). This magnificent granite block was erected at the temple of Amun on Jebel Barkal, a hill near Napata, Piye's capital. Napata lay just west of the Fourth Cataract. Later, the Nubians moved their capital to Meroë (MER oh ee), between the Fifth and Sixth Cataracts. While centered in Meroë, the kingdom of Kush entered its golden age.

Far to the southeast of Meroë, another great civilization flourished in the ancient city of Aksum, high in the Ethiopian mountains, between Gondar and the Red Sea. Here another carved stele, conveniently

> A stele is a stone column, plaque, or marker bearing carved or painted inscriptions.

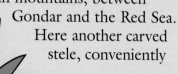

left behind by the great Aksumite king Ezana (e ZAH nah), has helped historians form a picture of long-ago events.

Just as the Egyptians and Nubians built their great monuments in stone, so did the Aksumite, or Ethiopian, kings leave behind massive stone steles, cities, churches, monasteries, and palaces. Some are made from rock and decorated with colorful, painted images drawn from the dawn of Christianity. They are used today much as they were in ancient times. Others rise in towers and battlements as splendid as any medieval castle in Europe. Still others lie in ruins, mysterious testaments to ancient splendor.

For decades, historians have debated whether Egypt, Kush, and Aksum were really African kingdoms. As one historian has asked,

"They are *in* Africa, but are they *of* Africa?" In their discussion, historians focus on people's spiritual beliefs, patterns of culture and migration, and ideas of kingship and statehood. Each kingdom shows many foreign influences. There are also many differences between the kingdoms in religious beliefs, architecture, and culture. Yet current research is gradually revealing powerful connections between these ancient kingdoms and the regions of Africa that surrounded them. The flow of goods and ideas back and forth between these regions has created an indestructible web, woven over centuries of time, that inevitably links northeast Africa with the rest of the continent.

Egypt—The Eighteenth Dynasty

Hatshepsut: The Queen King

The god Amun-Re (AH muhn re), Lord of Thebes and ruler of Egypt, called together all the gods, for he wished to beget a child to rule over the lands of the Nile. Thoth, god of wisdom, selected the lovely queen Ahmose (ah MOH se), wife of King Thutmose (tut MOH se) I, to be the bearer of this child.

Amun found Ahmose as she slept in her palace. She was like a jewel in her beauty, and the chamber in which she slept was like the setting for that jewel, and her couch was in the form of a fierce lion. In majesty and beauty, Amun appeared before her, and her heart was filled with joy. From this union between god and mortal was the child Hatshepsut conceived.

And Amun said to Ahmose, "Hatshepsut shall be the name of this my daughter, whom I have placed in thy body. She shall exercise the king-ship in this whole land. My soul is hers, my bounty is hers, my crown is hers, that she may lead the Two Lands."

Then Amun-Re commanded the god Khnum, the creator, to fashion his daughter. Khnum then seated himself before a potter's wheel and fash-ioned from clay first Hatshepsut and then her *ka* (kah), her spirit. And

HATSHEPSUT

close by knelt the birth goddess Heqt, who infused the clay with life. And Khnum gave to Hatshepsut all health, all lands, all countries, all people, that she might be King of Upper and Lower Egypt, of South and North, just as her father Amun-Re had commanded.

The child Hatshepsut grew to maidenhood. To look upon her was to behold great beauty. Like a god's was her form; like a god's was her splendor, and she made her divine form flourish and bloom. And Her Majesty journeyed to the north country, to the city of Heliopolis, where she was to be crowned by the gods.

To Heliopolis came Amun, her father, Lord of Thebes; Atum, Lord of Heliopolis; Khnum, Lord of the Cataract; and all the gods of Upper and Lower Egypt, their images born on the shoulders of their priests in a triumphal procession. They said, "Welcome, daughter of Amun-Re. Thou hast seen thy work in this land. Thou shalt set it in order, thou shalt restore that which has gone to ruin, thou shalt make thy monuments in this house. Thou shalt place food and drink on the offering tables of Amun-Re, who begat thee, and thou shalt pass through the land and embrace many nations. Egypt shall be filled with thy children's children, in number like grains of corn.

"The gods praise thee, for their heart hath given understanding to the life which they have fashioned. They shall set thy boundary as far as the breadth of heaven, as far as the limits of the twelfth hour of the night."

Hatshepsut received from the gods the red crown of Lower Egypt and the white crown of Upper Egypt. And now, adorned as a king and bearing all the royal insignia, she was proclaimed in the presence of her

▲ The name Hatshepsut means "Foremost of Noble Ladies." Like the names of all pharaohs, it is always framed by a cartouche, or symbol for a protective rope. The last hieroglyphics were carved in A.D. 394, soon after a Christian Roman emperor ordered the closing of all pagan temples. Thereafter, the key to the language remained lost until 1761, when a French priest guessed that the cartouches might frame royal names. In 1799 an inscribed stone now known as the Rosetta Stone was found by soldiers on Napoleon's campaign to Egypt. The stone was inscribed with the same text three times: in Egyptian hieroglyphics, in a cursive script, and in ancient Greek. By comparing the ancient Greek inscription and the names inside the cartouches, the scholar Jean François Champollion was able to decipher the hieroglyphics.

mortal father, the pharaoh Thutmose I, before the court at the temple of Deir el-Bahri (DER el-BAHR ee). Thutmose said to the members of the court, "This is my daughter, Hatshepsut, the living. I have appointed her as my successor to my glorious throne. She it is who shall lead you. Ye shall hear her words and be united at her command. Those who worship her shall live, those who blaspheme her shall die."

The gathered multitude kissed the earth that Hatshepsut's feet had trodden and rejoiced, praising all the gods of Upper and Lower Egypt. And they went forth and proclaimed the news to the people, who leaped and danced for the joy of their hearts. And they recognized Hatshepsut, their queen, and proclaimed her royal names, and called her divine, the daughter of a god, daughter of Amun-Re.

Now at this time, Her Majesty Queen Hatshepsut consulted the oracle of Amun-Re. The oracle commanded the great queen, ruler of the two lands, to seek out the ways to the land of Punt, far to the south, for no one of Egypt had yet trod this land. Yet it was known by hearsay, from those men who sold and bought goods across the Nubian deserts, that great marvels came from this land.

Queen Hatshepsut bowed to the god, saying, "I will command my army to tread these lands and to explore the waters of inaccessible channels, and I will reach the terraces of myrrh in the land of Punt and return with great gifts."

◀ This statue of Hatshepsut was found in a quarry near her temple at Deir el-Bahri.

Hair was important to the Egyptians, and they took great care of it. Children are almost always shown wearing their hair tied in one or two side locks, with the rest of the skull clean-shaven. Both men and women wore wigs made of thousands of human hairs, often woven in complex braids and strands. Here, Queen Kawit of Dynasty II has her hair dressed by a servant.

The queen's vessels set sail soon thereafter, journeying in peace to the land of Punt, according to the command of Amun-Re. And when they arrived, the lords of Punt bowed their heads to receive this army of the queen. "Why have ye come thither, unto this land, which thy people know not?" they asked. "Did ye come down upon the ways of heaven, or did ye sail upon the waters? Is there no way that we may reach Her Majesty, that we may live by the breath she breathes?"

As the Egyptians had arrived in peace, so they left in peace. Their ships were heavily laden with the marvels of the country of Punt, with fragrant woods, heaps of myrrh resin, and myrrh trees, which the sailors took by their roots and carried on board, to be set in the soil of Egypt. They took with them ebony and pure ivory, gold, cinnamon wood, incense, and eye cosmetic; apes, monkeys, dogs, ostrich feathers, giraffes, and skins of the southern panther. They took natives and their children, who wished to see the great land of

Egypt. Never was brought the like of this for any king of Egypt who had reigned since the beginning of time.

Hatshepsut's army returned to the kingdom in great glory, and she announced this to the people, saying, "I shine forever through that which my father, the god Amun-Re, hath desired." Then the queen ordered the myrrh trees to be planted at the temple of Amun-Re, in the garden that she called "Punt in Egypt." This done, she began to fulfill the other commands of the god's oracle and ordered her people to restore the great temples of Cusae (KOO seye) and Pakht, and others that had been destroyed by the warring Asiatics.

In the fifteenth year of the great queen Hatshepsut's reign, she commanded two great obelisks to be made for the temple of Amun-Re at Karnak. Senenmut, the queen's favorite adviser, was in command of the laborers, and he caused them to dig the granite at Aswan, a work achieved in a mere seven months. They carried the great stones to Thebes on barges drawn by a fleet of 27 galleys and rowed by the strength of 800 men.

"Hear ye!" cried the queen to the assembled people when the obelisks were raised. "As I sat in the palace, I remembered him who fashioned me, and my heart led me to make for him these obelisks, whose points mingle with heaven. I thought how the people would say my mouth was excellent by reason of that which issued from it."

And the queen commanded her people to take care of these great structures and all others that she had built and restored. And on the obelisks, the queen had her scribes write: "Let him who shall hear me not say I boast idly, but say, 'How like her it is who is truthful in the sight of her father, the god Amun-Re.' For he it is who has caused me to do all these things, to journey to the land of Punt and to restore the temples, as he commanded. I have no enemy in any land; all countries are my subjects. The lord Amun has made my

boundaries the extremities of heaven; the circuit of the sun has labored for me. I am Amun's daughter, who glorifies him with life, stability, and happiness. Upon the throne of all the living, I live, like Amun-Re, forever."

The ancient Egyptians called the delta region, roughly from Memphis to the Mediterranean coast, Lower Egypt. The Nile Valley from Memphis to Aswan was called Upper Egypt. Upper Egypt was divided into 22 *nomes*, or provinces, each governed by a *nomarch*, or administrator. Each *nome* had is own symbol, usually an animal such as the ibis or hare. In Lower Egypt, 20 *nomes* were created at a much later date. From about 1570 to 1070 B.C., Egypt's boundaries extended well into Palestine and Syria. The Nubian kingdom of Kush extended along the Nile Valley from Aswan south to Napata, and later to Meroë. At times, Nubia, or Kush, was ruled by Egypt, but from 747 to 646 B.C., Kushite kings ruled Egypt. Throughout their long history, the two kingdoms remained closely related through trade and culture. ▶

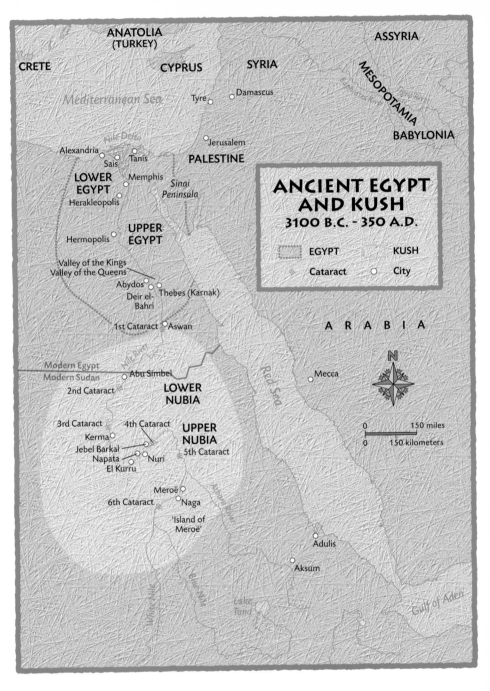

ANCIENT EGYPT
AND KUSH
3100 B.C. – 350 A.D.

EGYPT   KUSH

Cataract   ○ City

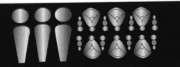

The Queen's Own Story

The African queen Hatshepsut reigned in Egypt from about 1498 to 1483 B.C. Her story is taken from inscriptions on the walls of her great funerary temple at Deir el-Bahri, across the Nile from Luxor. The inscriptions, which are depicted in wall paintings and hieroglyphics, were collected by many students of Egyptian history and translated by the eminent Egyptologist James Henry Breasted. From them, a glimmer of the intelligent, strong-willed, arrogant, and politically shrewd queen emerges. This is, of course, exactly the image that Hatshepsut wished to leave. Like all other rulers of ancient Egypt, she dictated to her scribes what she wished to be known.

Many of Hatshepsut's claims in these inscriptions can be confirmed. She did promote and finance an extraordinary expedition to the land of Punt—the first time the ancient Egyptians undertook a peaceful

◄ Hatshepsut's expedition to Punt is represented in great detail in a relief in her temple. Here, Ati, the obese wife of the ruler of Punt, joins a procession of gift-bearers for the expedition.

journey of exploration. She also repaired and expanded many temples and raised the giant obelisks at the temple of Karnak. It is also probable that she herself led a conquering expedition to Nubia. Her reign is generally considered, however, to have been mainly peaceful—a break from the great period of warlike expansion that had preceded it.

Much of Hatshepsut's story remains a mystery, however. Sadly, the temple reliefs were severely damaged, possibly by Hatshepsut's stepson, Thutmose III, who was his stepmother's rival for the throne. Some sections are missing, and historians can only guess at their content.

Fortunately, Professor Breasted was able to use a more ancient papyrus text to piece the story together. According to the text, known as the Papyrus Westcar after the archaeologist who found it, the sun-god Re had once ruled all of Egypt. In order to enhance their power and their claims to the throne, pharaohs from about 2,500 B.C. onward claimed direct

descent from Re and a mortal mother. Later, so the legend goes, Amun, the son of Re, succeeded him as ruler of Egypt, and the pharaohs then claimed descent through Amun. The story became standard and was depicted with the same inscriptions and paintings on most of the kings' tombs.

Hatshepsut claims that she was conceived when Amun visited her mother, Ahmose, at night. This charming version of Hatshepsut's divine birth is, however, a mere repetition of the ancient folk tale. In fact, Breasted determined that her inscriptions are almost identical to portions of the Papyrus Westcar, which refer to events that took place 1,000 years earlier.

Very strict rules governed who could legitimately rule Egypt. Egyptian men could claim the throne only by marriage to a high-ranking princess. To achieve this, men often married their sisters, and fathers their daughters. It was, however, extremely difficult and very rare for a woman to rule Egypt. Extraordinary events must have taken place in order for Hatshepsut to make

The Egyptians believed that a life force called the *ka* gave the body energy. The *ka* stayed with a body from birth through death and into the afterlife. The *ka* was represented as an exact double of a living person in drawings and figurines found in tombs and temples. Many other African cultures also believe in such a life force.

a legitimate claim to the throne and then hold on to her power.

Hatshepsut's own inscriptions reveal an almost desperate insistence on her right to the throne, as though it were threatened at every moment. The story of the divine birth, for example, had always applied to men, and Hatshepsut had to twist things a little in order to make her story fit. For example, in the paintings showing the god Khnum fashioning Hatshepsut and her *ka*, or spirit, from clay, the two babies are male! Was appearing "male" the only way that Hatshepsut could legitimately claim the throne? Several portraits of the queen show her wearing the traditional kilt, double crown, false beard, and royal insignia of a king or pharaoh. She also took all the traditional titles of a king—an unheard-of event for a woman in Egyptian history.

Throughout her story, Hatshepsut claims special connections with the gods. Apparently they had preordained her to rule Egypt even before her birth and had selected Ahmose as the most suitable mother for this divine child. And, Hatshepsut claims, the gods themselves

THE DIVINE KINGSHIP

The idea of "divine kingship" may have come to Egypt from African chiefs, or kings. They were believed to have special powers that made them responsible for rain, crops, fertility, and health—in short, for life and death. They were also the source of justice, creativity, and understanding. Such leaders were often thought to be gods who had become men and would become gods again after death. Menes (or Narmer) dammed the Nile to control its flood waters, leading to the development of better technology and higher living standards. To the Egyptians, this must have seemed like a miracle, due solely to the magical powers of their king.

had crowned her when she journeyed north to Heliopolis.

Such statements were routine for the rulers of ancient Egypt. Yet historians believe that Hatshepsut may have used them as political "propaganda," written to reinforce publicly what must have been a shaky claim to the throne. In the same way, although Hatshepsut certainly attended a crowning ceremony, the entire description of her coronation at

the court is a complete fiction. It is copied, word for word, from the account of the coronation of Amenemhet (ah MEN e met) II, who ruled Egypt 400 years earlier.

There is no question that Hatshepsut was a great queen—or pharaoh. But why did she have to resort to such falsehoods in the great monuments that were to preserve her history forever? The answer to this question can be found in the complex political situation that Hatshepsut inherited when she came to the throne.

◄ The pharaohs celebrated their reign with an important festival called *sed*, intended to ensure that the pharaoh could still continue his sacred duties. During *sed*, the king was honored by his people and had to run between stone cairns that symbolized the boundaries of Egypt. Here Hatshepsut, portrayed as a man and holding the sacred flail, performs her *sed* ritual.

have been deliberately removed and hacked to pieces in her own tomb and on many other monuments.

Even more puzzling are the two burial places Hatshepsut had constructed for herself. One tomb was in a valley far to the west of Thebes, and the other is her famed monument at Deir el-Bahri. But in both places only an empty coffin, or sarcophagus, has been found. Was Hatshepsut ever buried in either of these tombs? Were they vandalized and robbed at a later date, as happened with many of ancient Egypt's

monuments? Or was her body removed by political rivals who sought to destroy all trace of her?

These questions have caused much feuding among experts trying to unravel the mysteries of Hatshepsut's life. It is clear from various inscriptions that Thutmose II was the son of Thutmose I by a second wife—in other words, Thutmose II was Hatshepsut's half brother. As Hatshepsut was the royal heiress, claims to the throne could be legitimized only by marrying her, and Thutmose II did just that. He reigned for about 20 years, leaving the throne to Thutmose III, his son by another wife. Since Thutmose III was only a boy at the time of his father's death, it was natural for Hatshepsut—his stepmother—to reign with him as coregent until he was old enough to rule Egypt himself.

Hatshepsut, however, did not give up the throne to her stepson but held her position long after Thutmose III could have become pharaoh. In this, she appears to have been iron-willed and ruthless. Almost certainly she used the support and probable

Around 3000 B.C., the kings of Upper Egypt wore a white crown, or *hedjet*. Kings of Lower Egypt wore a red crown, or *deshret*. When Menes (or Narmer), king of Upper Egypt, united the two regions into one kingdom, the crowns were combined to form the double crown, called the "Two Mighty Ones," or *pschent*. For 30 centuries, the kings of Egypt called themselves the Lords of the Two Lands. Here, the personifications of Lower Egypt (*left*) and Upper Egypt (*right*) crown Pharaoh Ptolemy VI (180–145 B.C.) with the double crown. ▶

◀ This ostrich shell, decorated with antelope figures, was found in an Egyptian grave dating from the predynastic period between 3600 and 3400 B.C.. The shells were rarely used as containers. More often, they were carved into flat beads.

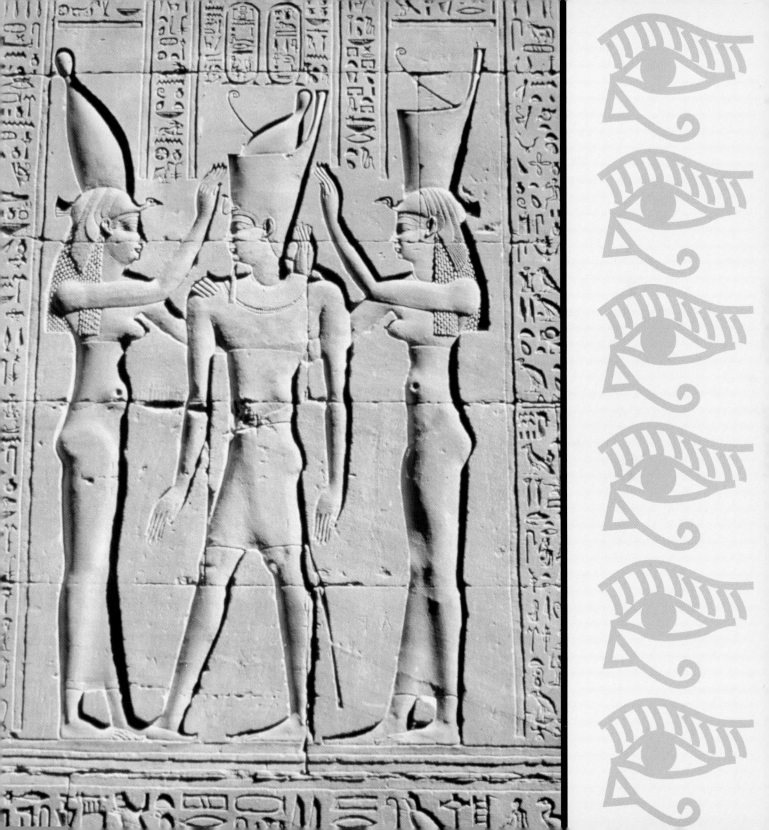

intrigues of her various advisers to maintain her grip on the throne.

Hatshepsut took every opportunity to insist that her father, Thutmose I, had appointed her his successor, even building a shrine for him in her own temple. Thutmose III, however, made equal claims. In the walls of the Karnak temple, built near Thebes during his reign, an inscription says, "I am his son, whom he commanded that I should be upon the throne . . . There is no lie therein." Like Hatshepsut, Thutmose III also claimed to have been selected to be king by the god Amun-Re. Thutmose was chosen during a religious festival at which an image of the god, born by a priest, halted before the young prince and led

Dynasty 18 rulers abandoned pyramid tombs and built their burial chambers in the Valley of the Kings. The pharaohs Menhutohep, Hatshepsut, and Thutmose III also built funerary temples at Deir el-Bahri, a deep bay in the cliffs. The most spectacular of these, shown here, was designed for Hatshepsut by her favorite minister, Senenmut. It is considered one of the architectural wonders of the world. ▼

him to the "Station of the King"—the place where the reigning pharaoh stood during the ceremony.

Was there a tremendous power struggle between Hatshepsut and Thutmose III? Or were such rival claims simply part of the normal pattern of Egyptian kingship? Were the priests who favored Thutmose III involved in a scheme to bring him to the throne? And what of Senenmut, Hatshepsut's most powerful minister? He played a pivotal role in her life and was heavily involved in all her many building projects. He also reared and tutored Hatshepsut's daughter, Nefru-Re, heiress to the throne, but then he seems to vanish from history. Some experts believe that Senenmut might have been Hatshepsut's lover. Perhaps she hoped that he would eventually marry her daughter and thus become pharaoh himself.

It is doubtful whether these secrets will ever be revealed. Hatshepsut died about 1483 B.C. It is not known how she died. She may have been murdered by Thutmose III, who went on to become one of Egypt's greatest

pharaohs. It seems that after Hatshepsut's death, Thutmose III may have ordered his workers to hack out her name from every monument where it occurred and to replace it with his own, or those of his father and grandfather. Almost every statue of Hatshepsut was smashed to pieces and pounded to dust. And the tombs of Senenmut and all of Hatshepsut's ministers and advisers were plundered, and their faces destroyed.

These actions had severe consequences. The ancient Egyptians believed that sculptured and painted images had magical qualities and provided the dead with the means to eternal life, such as food, weapons, clothing, and tools. If the images were destroyed, the spirit of the dead could no longer live in the hereafter and would die forever.

Some historians believe that Thutmose III could only have acted out of hatred and jealousy.

▲ Many statues depict Hatshepsut's chief adviser, Senenmut, with her baby daughter, Nefru-Re. Senenmut bore many titles. He was Chief Architect and Overseer of Works, Chief Steward of Amun, and Overseer of the Granaries, Fields, Cattle, Gardens, and Weavers of Amun. He was the head of government, and only the chief priest of Amun was equal to him in religious affairs.

◀ Thutmose III was a great soldier and athlete, renowned as a crack shot with a bow and arrow. Called the Napoleon of ancient Egypt by historian James Henry Breasted, the king launched 17 campaigns against western Asia, capturing 350 cities. In this wall painting at a shrine at Deir el-Bahri, Thutmose makes offerings to Amun. Thutmose III lived well into his eighties. In 1881, his mummy was found together with 40 others in a deep shaft tomb at Deir el-Bahri. They had been placed there by priests of Dynasty 21 as protection against grave robbers.

By destroying all the images of Hatshepsut, he "murdered" her spirit and dealt her and her supporters the final deathblow. Other historians think that Thutmose III may have been forced to destroy the images in order to reinstate himself as the rightful heir to the throne and to reestablish his link with his grandfather, Thutmose I, who was revered as a powerful leader.

Here and there, in the darkest, most hidden corners of her shrines, the undamaged name and image of Hatshepsut can still be found. Was this an accident? Or did Egypt's greatest pharaoh secretly bow to Hatshepsut, his stepmother? Recent discoveries seem to indicate that the damage to Hatshepsut's names and images was done late in Thutmose's reign, and may have been the work of someone else altogether. We may never know the truth. But for centuries to come, the story of Hatshepsut will echo in the abandoned stone monuments that haunt the banks of the Nile.

These glass containers, made by craftspeople of Dynasty 18, held oils and cosmetics. The jug bears the name of Thutmose III and is one of the earliest examples of Egyptian glass. ▼

Kush—The Nubian Kingdom

Piye: Prince of Cunning

King Kashta had died. Now his son, Piye, who had not yet come of age, would be king of Kush. And Piye took on this role with courage and wisdom, for he had been well trained by the priests of Amun. "Ye shall rule Kush and Egypt as wisely as thy father has done," the high priest had said, "and thy sons shall rule after thee."

The young Piye grew up in the palace at Napata. Before him flowed the smooth waters of the Nile, making the fertile valley green with barley and wheat; behind him burned the harsh sands of the great Nubian desert. Piye learned to hunt the lion, the leopard, the elephant, and the ostrich, for the prince was tall, strong, and brave. He learned to ride horses fearlessly and to love them just as he loved his people.

In the first month of his twenty-first year, when Piye had become king, his vassals from Upper Egypt brought grave news to the palace at Napata. A prince of northern Egypt, they said, had conquered the kings of the entire delta to the west, south, and east of the Nile. The rulers of all the walled cities were as dogs at the heels of this prince, Tefnakht (tef NAHKT) by name. Each had opened the doors of his city to the warrior for fear of his conquering might. Tefnakht had thus become regent of all of Lower Egypt and of the northern portion of Upper Egypt. Only the city of Herakleopolis stood fast against him, besieged though it was by Tefnakht and all his vassal princes.

Piye's messengers awaited the king's command. Surely, they thought, their king would rise up against Tefnakht and defeat him, thus bringing all of Egypt into the Kushite realm. But Piye merely smiled. It would be foolhardy, he said, to send his army into the swampy delta where Tefnakht fought. Far better, he said, to wait until the Egyptian prince came farther south, where he would make an easy target for Piye's forces.

Before long, a second plea came from Piye's officers in the north. "Wilt thou be silent," they asked, "while Tefnakht advances his conquest throughout the realm and finds none who can withstand him?" Namlot, the king of Hermopolis, had submitted to Tefnakht, the officers reported. "Behold," they said, "how Namlot follows at Tefnakht's heels and gives to him all the gifts that he desires."

At this news, Piye commanded his officers to proceed north again, to join with the Nubian soldiers already in Egypt, and to besiege Namlot's city of Hermopolis. "Hasten into battle," he told his trusted men. "Surround the city and capture its people. Let not the peasants go forth to the field, and let not the plowmen plow."

While Piye's men hurried north, he dispatched a second army into Egypt, to support his men in the siege of Hermopolis. The soldiers praised their king.

"It is thy valor that gives us might," they cried, "and thy name that gives us strength." The soldiers left in great haste, sailing down the Nile to the holy city of Thebes, temple of Amun. There, they purified themselves in the river and prayed to Amun for strength and courage, for it was in the shadow of Amun's sword that they would fight.

When they left Thebes, they came upon Tefnakht's fleet of ships sailing upstream, bearing many able soldiers, sailors, and commanders of the northern lands. But Piye's men set upon the enemy in fury. They caused a great slaughter and captured the survivors and their ships, which were sent south to Napata.

Piye's forces continued to the north. At Hermopolis, they heard that Namlot had forsaken his own city in order to fight for his new lord, Tefnakht, in the siege of Herakleopolis. Piye's men hurried north to Herakleopolis. Once again, they entered the

◀ Two sacred cobras on the forehead of this Kushite king distinguish him from Egyptian kings, who wore only one. The great thumb ring was used for pulling a bow string, recalling the fame of the Kushite archers.

fray with their king's name upon their lips and soundly defeated their enemy. They killed many of Tefnakht's men and his horses and pursued Tefnakht and his remaining soldiers far to the north. Namlot himself escaped and returned to Hermopolis to protect his city, whereupon the Nubian commanders also returned there to besiege the city, as Piye had commanded.

When the news reached Piye that Tefnakht and some of his forces had escaped to the north, he was filled with anger. "As Re loves me, and as my father Amun loves me," he raged, "I will myself go northward that I may bring an end to Tefnakht's conquests forever."

When Piye's forces to the north heard of their king's anger, they fought ever more valiantly to conquer one city after the other. At Tetehen they breached the walls with a battering ram. At Hatbenu, the army stormed the city. But still Piye was not satisfied. He himself took command of the siege of Hermopolis, where Namlot trembled in fear. He ordered the city walls to be enclosed by high banks of mud, and his archers raised a great tower from which they could shoot over the walls.

Hermopolis lay under siege for almost five months. It stank from refuse and from the decaying bodies of the dead. The people were starving. At last, the city surrendered. Messengers came out, bearing gold, costly clothing, and the diadem that had adorned King Namlot's head. But Piye remained unmoved. Then Namlot sent out his own queen, Nestent, to plead with Piye's women for deliverance. "We come to you, O king's wives, daughters, and sisters," she said, "that ye may beg your king to be lenient with us." This the women did, and Piye's heart softened, and he accepted the surrender of

Namlot and the city of Hermopolis. Namlot presented Piye with silver, gold, lapis lazuli, malachite, bronze, and other rare gems. Piye filled his treasury with this bounty and presented a good portion of it to the estate of Amun. He entered the city in triumph and took it for his own.

Such was the might of Piye that now the ruler of Herakleopolis, which had been besieged by Tefnakht, came to greet him and to praise him for deliverance. Piye resumed his journey northward, and one by one the cities to the west of the Nile surrendered when they saw his forces.

When Piye arrived at Memphis, however, he saw that the city was well fortified and the people safe within. The mighty walls were protected on the east by the high waters of the Nile. First, Piye demanded surrender, promising the safety of the people. The people of Memphis made no answer but closed their gates and sent out a small force against His Majesty's army. The force was easily routed.

That night, as Piye's forces rested, Tefnakht secretly entered the city and beseeched his forces, which numbered some 8,000 men, to hold fast while he returned to the north for reinforcements. "Behold," he told them, "the granaries are overflowing. Ye have weapons of war, and cattle, and the treasury is filled with silver, gold, honey, incense, and oil. Wait but a few days until I return." Then Tefnakht mounted his horse and raced to the north.

Meanwhile, Piye and his officers debated how they could take Memphis. Some wished to attack the city and break down its walls, others to besiege it and cause its people to starve. But Piye raged against the city like a panther, for he would fulfill the command of Amun. He saw that the prows of the ships

moored in the harbor rode so high that they were made fast to the roofs of the houses within the city walls. Thus Piye ordered his men to attack the harbor and to bring him all the ferryboats and cargo ships. He lined up these vessels so that their prows reached the top of the eastern wall and they formed a bridge and a firm footing for his soldiers. "Forward!" he exhorted his men. "Mount the walls!" And his men ran along the ships and over the walls and entered the city.

And thus, through the cunning of Piye, was Memphis captured. Now all the dynasts of the north came to Piye at Memphis and submitted to his rule. Even Tefnakht sent his messengers from the far-off delta island that was his refuge and beseeched Piye with flattery. "Be thou appeased!" he begged. "I have not beheld thy face for shame, I tremble at thy might, the fear of thee is in my bones. The year has undone me." He was ill, Tefnakht said, his head bare, his clothing in rags. Could not Piye forgive him and allow him to cleanse himself in a temple, where he would pledge an oath of allegiance?

To this, King Piye agreed, for it was the time of the floods, and to pursue Tefnakht into the delta was foolhardy. Now Piye, the black king, was pharaoh: lord of Kush and of all Egypt.

Then His Majesty's ships were laden with all the bounty of the north, and he sailed upstream with a glad heart. On the shores of the Nile the people jubilated. "O mighty, mighty ruler, Piye," they sang. "Thou makest bulls into women! Happy the heart of the mother who bore thee, and the man who begat thee. Thou art eternal and thy might endureth."

The Kushite Dynasty

Piye, the Kushite king, ruled Nubia for 31 years, from 747 to 716 B.C. The story of his extraordinary conquest of Egypt is taken almost word for word from his "victory stele." Piye was the first king of Egypt's 25th, or Kushite, dynasty, reigning over a region extending from Napata some 1,935 km (1,200 mi) north to Memphis, east to the Ethiopian mountains, and west into the Libyan desert.

Other inscriptions tell of Piye's predecessor and father, Kashta. Around 751 B.C., Kashta succeeded in conquering Upper Egypt as far as Aswan, when Lower Egypt was ruled by Osorkon III, a Libyan king. Osorkon's daughter was a "Wife of the God Amun," or chief female priest, at Thebes. Either Kashta or Piye forced her to adopt Piye's sister Amenirdis (ah MEN ihr dihs) I and give her a high position at the temple. Through this bond, the Kushite kings ensured their command over Thebes and the all-important temple of Amun.

Some scholars believe that Kashta may have been asked by the Egyptian priesthood to aid Upper Egypt

against the ever-growing power of the Libyan kings to the north. When the Libyans threatened to attack Egypt, Piye may have been obliged to fulfill his father's promise by sending his own military forces to help the Egyptians. In addition, Kush had been under Egyptian influence for more than 1,000 years and was thoroughly Egyptianized in most aspects of its culture. When Piye heard of the northern threats to Egyptian unity, his main aim may have been to rid Egypt of the foreign threat and restore the unity of the Two Lands. More likely, however, the Nubian king may have seized this moment to conquer Egypt for himself. Whatever Piye's motives were, he posed a serious threat to

> At about the time that Kashta was conquering Upper Egypt, Rome had just been founded.

Tefnakht, king of the delta region of Sais. Tefnakht organized the coalition of northern kings to stem the Nubian advance but was soundly defeated by Piye.

Piye's reign fell during the Third Intermediate Period (1069–525 B.C.)—a time of great turmoil that foreshadowed the future collapse of the kingdom. There had been a split between the northern power centers of Tanis (TAH nihs), on the eastern delta, and Thebes. There was also a rift between Tanis and Leontopolis, in the central delta. At one point, three men claimed to be king at the same time! This split led to two separate dynasties, the 22nd and 23rd, ruling simultaneously in different places.

Once Egypt had been conquered, Piye allowed the defeated kings, including Tefnakht, to resume

Piye's "victory stele" is the most detailed of any text yet found in Egypt or Nubia. The language is unusually poetic, describing Piye as "raging like a panther" and "descending upon his enemies like a cloudburst." From it we learn that Piye was a great lover of horses and cursed Namlot for letting his horses starve during the siege of Hermopolis. In the royal Kushite graveyard at El-Kurru, 24 horses were found buried in rows. They wore silver headbands and plume carriers and must have been the horses for the chariot teams of Piye and his successors.

Shabaka revived an ancient text known as the Memphite Theology. It recorded how the universe was created by the god Ptah. First, Ptah imagined everything in his heart, which Egyptians believed was the center of the intellect. Then he said aloud the names of the gods, temples, people, and other items necessary for life on earth, thus bringing them into being. This myth is similar to the Gospel of John in the New Testament of the Bible: "In the beginning was the Word, and the Word was with God, and the Word was God." The Australian aborigines also believe that things came into existence when their names were spoken or sung out.

governing their provinces while he returned to Napata. Almost as soon as Piye's back was turned, however, Tefnakht regained control of the delta region, or Lower Egypt, and became the first king of the 24th Dynasty. His seven or eight years of rule in the north overlapped with Piye's reign in the south.

When Tefnakht died, his son Bekenrenef claimed his father's royal titles. Piye was succeeded by his brother Shabaka (716–702 B.C.). Bekenrenef continued his father's campaigns but was crushed—in fact, burned alive—by Shabaka. The Kushite king then moved his capital from Napata 800 km (500 mi) north to Thebes so that he could more effectively govern the kingdom of Egypt and keep an eye on the rebellious delta princes. Because he reigned from the Egyptian city of Thebes and not from the Nubian capital of Napata, Shabaka is sometimes listed as the first king of the 25th Dynasty. He is known for his vast building projects, mainly in connection with the Amun cult at Thebes but also at other major religious centers, such as Memphis and Abydos (AH bih dohs).

Shabaka reigned for 14 years. During this time, the Assyrians were expanding their empire ever eastward and had besieged Jerusalem. To prevent their entry into Egypt, Shabaka and his troops rushed to break the siege and were granted victory by a "miracle"— a plague that killed 15,000 Assyrians overnight. Shabaka was succeeded by Piye's son Shebitku (702–690 B.C.), followed shortly after by Piye's second son, Taharka (690–665 B.C.), who was only 25 when he came to the throne.

Famine, drought, and disease had plagued Egypt for years. But the beginning of Taharka's reign in 690 B.C. was blessed by a massive flooding of the Nile. The water level at Karnak, near Thebes, rose to an amazing 90 m

"The flood penetrated the hills of Upper Egypt, it overtopped the mounds of Lower Egypt, and the land became a primordial ocean. . . . Moreover, the sky rained in Nubia. . . . Every man had abundance of everything, Egypt was in happy festival."
—Taharka's description of a Nile flood

(300 ft). This event, combined with a rare period of good rainfall in Nubia, enhanced the new pharaoh's public esteem. Surely, the people believed, his reign would be blessed by the gods.

But it was not to be so. For Taharka's reign was also a time of almost continuous confrontation with the Assyrians. To deal with the Asian threat, Taharka moved his capital from Thebes to Tanis, in the eastern delta. When the Assyrian armies had temporarily withdrawn, the delta princes plotted with Taharka to restore him to power. But the Assyrians got wind of the rebellion and promptly killed most of the princes. Taharka lost the city of Memphis twice, narrowly escaping with his life, and had to flee south to Napata, where he died in 664 B.C.

Taharka's is the name most frequently associated with the Kushite Dynasty. Like Shabaka, he too was a great builder. He built or restored temples throughout Egypt and Kush. At Jebel Barkal, he copied the famous temple of Rameses II at Abu Simbel, cutting from the living rock an even larger, more imposing version of the original. At Kawa, about 190 km (120 mi) north of Napata, he built a huge temple on the site of a ruin he had noticed on his way to Egypt. An army of engineers, builders, and craftsmen erected solid sandstone walls covered with gold leaf and surrounded the magnificent building with gardens, vineyards, and an artificial lake. This temple to the gods was to be Taharka's greatest landmark.

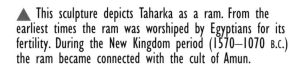
▲ This sculpture depicts Taharka as a ram. From the earliest times the ram was worshiped by Egyptians for its fertility. During the New Kingdom period (1570–1070 B.C.) the ram became connected with the cult of Amun.

▲ Taharka's gold ring, incised with the magical symbol of an eye, was found in his tomb at Nuri, near Napata.

Taharka was succeeded by his nephew, Tanutamun (tah nut AH-mun), who reigned from 664 to 656 B.C. This Kushite king had dreamed of two snakes rising up, one on each side of him. The dream was officially interpreted to mean that Tanutamun would take Egypt from the Assyrians and unite the kingdom once more. He swept north from Napata, recapturing Aswan, Thebes, and even Memphis from the Assyrians. Tanutamun must have believed that the gods were with him, but his success was short-lived. This time, the Assyrians brought down their considerable might against him. In an unprecedented and shocking move, they sacked and pillaged Thebes, "city of the thousand gates," and all its holy temples.

Tanutamun fled before the Assyrians and escaped to Napata. Shortly after-wards, the delta princes in the north managed to oust the Assyrians from Egypt. But to them, Nubia still posed a real threat. In 593 B.C. the Egyptians attacked Nubia and captured Napata. The period of Nubian domination of Egypt had come to an end.

Ancient and New Prejudices

The construction of the Aswan High Dam in the 1960s caused a flurry of archaeological activity in the region and led to new discoveries about the ancient civilizations of Nubia, or Kush, as it was called. These efforts preserved part of Nubia's history and uncovered much new information.

Interest in Nubia, or Kush, was not new, however. The region has had a hold on the western imagination for centuries. The ancient Greeks and Romans thought that Nubia was one of the greatest civilizations of the world. Although very few Greeks or Romans ever traveled there, they knew that inexhaustible supplies of gold, ebony, ivory, cattle, slaves, ostrich feathers, and panther skins, as well as exotic luxuries such as frankin-cense and plant oils, came from the mysterious region to the south of

45

◄ Archaeologists
on a pinnacle at
Jebel Barkal
enjoy a view
of millet fields
and groves
of date palms
overlying the
site of ancient
Napata, near
the Nile.

Herodotus wrote the first European account of Nubia, or *Aethiopia* (not to be confused with today's Ethiopia) as he called it, in about 430 B.C. The next mention of Nubia comes 400 years later, in a book by the Roman historian, Diodorus Siculus. In 7 B.C., the Greek historian Strabo described the region and people's customs there in his *Geography*. In his *Natural History*, the Roman author Pliny relied on accounts of Roman troops sent to Nubia around A.D. 61 for his information.

Egypt. From the same region came dark-skinned, mercenary warriors whose skill with the bow and arrow was unsurpassed. To Europeans, Nubia was a kingdom of extraordinary wealth and power.

The Greek historian Herodotus, who traveled as far as Aswan, was imaginative in his reports about the kingdom of Kush. He described the Nubians, or Kushites, as the "tallest and handsomest" people he had ever seen. They lived to be 120 years old on a diet of boiled meat and milk, he reported, and they carved their temples from a single stone. Their queen, he said, traveled in a wheeled palace, drawn by 20 elephants.

Other writers of ancient times added further snippets of information about Nubia.

Nubian (Sudanese) camel drivers ride past 2,500-year-old royal tombs near Jebel Barkal. Long after the Egyptians had stopped building pyramids, the Nubians were building small steep-sided pyramids with burial chambers located beneath them. There are more royal pyramids in the Sudan than in all of Egypt. A recent survey counted about 1 million ancient burial mounds! Only a few have been excavated.

Some were pure myth; others were fairly accurate descriptions of the land and people. But it was not until the nineteenth century that Europeans developed enough interest in the region to begin archaeological excavations there. In the 1990s, several major world museums mounted exhibitions of the more recent discoveries in the region. Yet, to the average person, Nubia remains virtually unknown, more remote and inaccessible today than it was in ancient times.

The lack of knowledge about Nubia, or Kush, may certainly be related to its remoteness from Europe. But the region's many different names, and those of its different kingdoms, also made—and still make— its geography and the exact location of its kingdoms confusing.

The ancient Egyptians called the region south of Aswan *Ta-Seti*, meaning "land of the bow," a reference to Nubia's famed archers. From about 2000 B.C., they called it Kush, the name that also appears in the Bible and is widely used by historians today. At one time, Nubia included all of present-day Sudan, Ethiopia, and Somalia. The Greeks and Romans called this region Aethiopia—a Greek word meaning "land of the burned faces" (a reference to the Nubians' dark skin)—and not to be confused with today's nation of Ethiopia, far to the east. Some historians refer to separate Nubian, or Kushite, kingdoms— Napata and Meroë— each centered around its capital city of the same name. Others include the city of Napata and all of Lower Nubia in the Kingdom of Kush and consider Upper Nubia the Kingdom of Meroë. In ancient times, these different names probably referred to different areas of Nubia, depending on the extent of geographical knowledge at the time. The name *Nubia* may be derived from the people known as the Noba, who inhabited the southern areas of the region. It may also stem from the-word *nub* which meant "slave" in a local language and was adopted by the Latin-speaking Romans. The term *Nubia* was first applied to the entire region by Europeans in the eighteenth century.

Nubia was a black African kingdom. This may also have slowed European interest in the region. After Nubia became Christianized in the sixth century A.D., there is not a single mention of its kingdoms in European reports until the late eighteenth century. The historian David Roberts believes that this neglect is a clear reflection of racial discrimination. Until recently, he says, the western mind found it impossible to believe that Africans could have developed the sophisticated cultures that flourished in Nubia for over 5,000 years. This trend in thinking continued through the early twentieth century. Even the eminent archaeologist George Reisner concluded that the kings whose tombs he excavated in the region must have been descendants of a Libyan—that is, a white—dynasty.

This racial bias was evident from the very first contact of Europeans with Nubia. There is, for example, a record of a Nubian queen's response to an inquiry from Alexander the Great, the Macedonian emperor who conquered Egypt in 332 B.C. Alexander wished to know more about Kush. The queen wrote to him, "Do not despise us for the color of our skin. In our souls we are brighter than the whitest of your people."

Most of what is known about ancient Nubia has been gleaned from the reports of other peoples, such as the Egyptians, Assyrians, Greeks, and Romans, who came either to trade or to conquer. Since the Nubians were among Egypt's most dire enemies, the pharaohs often referred to their southern neighbors as "vile" and "wretched" people. They drew images of Nubians on the soles of their sandals and under their footstools, where they could be symbolically crushed. Yet although the Kushite reign in Egypt lasted just over 60 years, the Nubian civilization far outlasted the Egyptian. It continued to flourish for another 1,000 years.

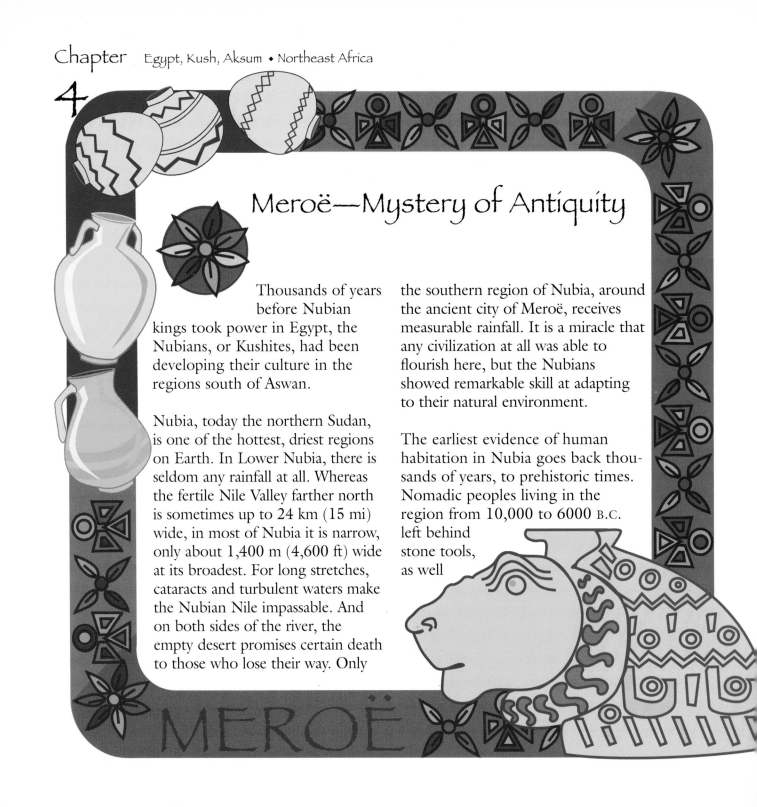

Meroë—Mystery of Antiquity

Thousands of years before Nubian kings took power in Egypt, the Nubians, or Kushites, had been developing their culture in the regions south of Aswan.

Nubia, today the northern Sudan, is one of the hottest, driest regions on Earth. In Lower Nubia, there is seldom any rainfall at all. Whereas the fertile Nile Valley farther north is sometimes up to 24 km (15 mi) wide, in most of Nubia it is narrow, only about 1,400 m (4,600 ft) wide at its broadest. For long stretches, cataracts and turbulent waters make the Nubian Nile impassable. And on both sides of the river, the empty desert promises certain death to those who lose their way. Only

the southern region of Nubia, around the ancient city of Meroë, receives measurable rainfall. It is a miracle that any civilization at all was able to flourish here, but the Nubians showed remarkable skill at adapting to their natural environment.

The earliest evidence of human habitation in Nubia goes back thousands of years, to prehistoric times. Nomadic peoples living in the region from 10,000 to 6000 B.C. left behind stone tools, as well

MEROË

as bone arrow- and harpoon-heads, and the oldest pottery yet found on African soil. These Negroid people hunted and gathered in the region, which was then much wetter than it is today. Gradually, as the area dried out and food became scarce, people were forced to settle along the banks of the Nile—the only place where crops could be grown and watered. They eventually developed villages and towns, and it is from these urban beginnings that the true Nubian culture emerged.

Between 3500 and 2800 B.C., people whom archaeologists have labeled the A-Group, for want of a better term, lived in Lower Nubia, between the First and Second Cataracts. These people were not Negroid but resembled Egyptians. The Egyptians frequently raided the territory inhabited by the A-Group. King Snefru of the 4th Dynasty (ca. 2500 B.C.), for example, bragged about a military campaign to Nubia that brought him a booty of 7,000 Nubian prisoners and 200,000 head of cattle!

Such Egyptian campaigns may have driven the A-Group people farther south. Around 2300 B.C. (near the close of the

Old Kingdom), two new peoples emerged in Nubia. One, known to archaeologists as the C-Group, is clearly distinguished from previous groups by its burial methods and pottery. The C-Group people portrayed cattle on pottery, on gravestones, in clay figures placed on graves, and in rock paintings and were clearly skilled cattle-breeders. Their area of settlement extended from Aswan to the Second Cataract.

The C-Group traded peacefully with the kingdom of Egypt for centuries. The Middle Kingdom pharaohs of the 11th and 12th Dynasties (2040–1782 B.C.), however, again attacked the south and eventually occupied Nubia as far as the Second Cataract. They built several colossal fortresses along the Nile, all within signaling distance of one another. These strongholds were designed to protect the desert and river trade routes from marauding desert nomads. They were also a defense against the other Nubian group that emerged at this time at Kerma, deep in Nubia

Cattle figurines were common among the C-group graves excavated at Aniba, in Lower Nubia. ▼

The Egyptians recorded the highest point of the Nile at their fortresses in Nubia. Some of the measurements they made are up to 8 m (26 ft) higher than the highest point reached by the Nile today.

between the Third and Fourth Cataracts.

After 1700 B.C., during the Second Intermediate Period of turmoil and conflict (1782–1570 B.C.), the Egyptians abandoned their Nubian forts along the Nile. Freed from Egyptian dominance, the Kerma culture was able to flourish as never before. Around this time, gold was discovered in the Nubian deserts. It formed the basis of trade between Egypt and Kerma, which developed into a wealthy and sophisticated city-state.

At Kerma, archaeologists found a king's grave or circular mound as wide across as a football field. It bears witness to Kerma's prosperity. The interior rooms of the tomb were brilliantly painted and filled with exquisite objects wrought of gold, bronze, and ivory. The king was laid out on a luxurious gold-covered bed. Over 300 well-dressed servants, concubines, and followers had been buried alive in the grave. They had chosen to die with their king.

Around 1500 B.C. the tide turned yet again when Egypt conquered most of Nubia, extending the southern frontier to Kurgus, between the Fourth and Fifth Cataracts. The great palace at Kerma was destroyed, and Nubia became a vassal of Egypt. Pharaoh Ahmose I (1570–1546 B.C.) installed a viceroy, or governor, known as the "King's Son of Kush," in Nubia. His main duty was to ensure the punctual delivery of tribute—mostly gold—from the Nubians to the Egyptians. Pharaoh Thutmose III collected about 250 kg (550 lbs) of gold annually, worth nearly $3 million today, from one Nubian province alone! He also took about 400 cattle as tribute each year, as well as slaves, minerals, ebony, ivory, ostrich feathers, and many other Nubian products.

During this period, Nubian princes were educated at the Egyptian court and became thoroughly Egyptianized. Gradually, as they returned to Nubia and as Egyptians settled in their vassal state, the distinctive Nubian culture seemed to fade. Egyptian architecture, customs,

clothing, and even the Egyptian language replaced those of the indigenous people. Many Nubians worked in the gold mines; others were mercenary soldiers or slaves for the Egyptians. Some reached high government or religious positions in Egypt. They worshiped Egyptian gods and used Egyptian hieroglyphics to inscribe their great deeds in stone.

For almost five centuries, Nubia's distinctive culture was eclipsed by Egypt. But in the thirteenth century B.C., after the reign of Rameses II, Egypt broke up into rival city-states and released its hold on Nubia. From about 1000 to about 850

▲ A Nubian slave girl carries a serving dish that rests on the head of a monkey. This wooden figure was made during Dynasty 18, sometime between 1390 and 1352 B.C.

B.C., Nubia seems to disappear from recorded history. Not a single inscription or text has been found that sheds light on this mysterious period. But when Nubia finally reemerges in recorded history, it is as the strong and prosperous kingdom of Kush, centered at Napata. Only a century after coming to power, the Kushite kings achieved their crowning triumph: the conquest of Egypt under their great leader, Piye.

The Iron City

The African kings of the Kushite dynasty in Egypt revered and preserved many ancient Egyptian traditions. They revived pyramid burials, which had ceased in Egypt centuries earlier. They ordered scribes to copy ancient

(next two pages) Scenes from the temple of Bewit el-Wali in Nubia show Amenope, the viceroy of Kush, receiving wild animals and other products as tribute from Nubia. He is also being rewarded by Pharaoh Rameses II with gold collars that resemble chains.

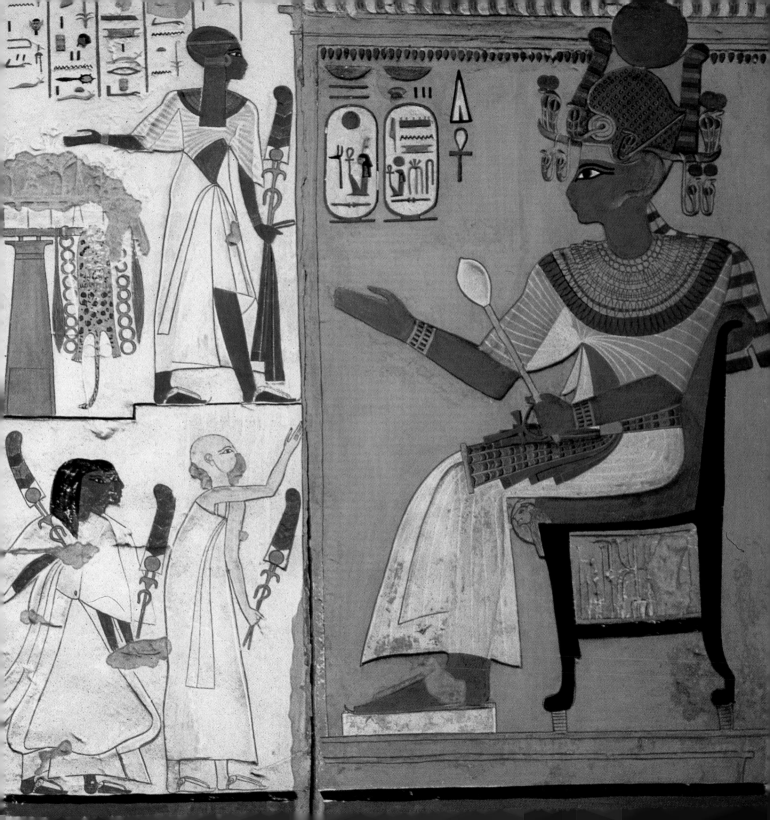

Egyptian texts that had long since fallen into disuse. Temples and monuments were repaired, and new ones built. And with their great temple at Jebel Barkal the Nubians rivaled the Egyptians in their cult of the god Amun.

After the Assyrian defeat of Tanutamun and the Egyptian sack of Napata, however, the Nubians retreated to safety deep within the heart of Kush. At some time during the sixth century B.C., they established their capital at Meroë, about 500 km (300 mi) south of Napata, between the Fifth Cataract and the merging of the Nile and the Atbara Rivers. After centuries of Egyptianization, it was at Meroë that the Kushite culture finally flowered again and came into its own.

Today a railroad runs close to the ruins of the ancient town of Meroë. One sees a few small temples and beyond them the vast stone platform that is thought to be the temple of the sun that Herodotus described in 430 B.C. A little farther are the ruins of the small pyramids in which nobles and wealthy individuals were buried, and beyond them lies the cemetery of the African kings and queens who ruled Meroë from 300 B.C. onward.

These few relics are all that remain of the Meroitic civilization. Through extensive research and excavation, however, specialists on Nubian history have begun to piece together the story of the thousand-year period when Meroë served as the Nubian, or Kushite, capital, and why the Nubians chose to move there from Napata in the first place.

Napata was located in a dry desert where the narrow Nile Valley limited cultivation. Meroë, on the other hand, lay in the well-watered triangle of land between the Nile and the Atbara rivers. Because of its location, it was often called the Island of Meroë. Although scarcely any rain fell in northern Nubia, Meroë lay within a southern region of tropical seasonal rainfall. The Meroites took advantage of the climate and built large rain collection pools and a complex system of irrigation canals. Instead of barren desert, grassy plains stretched on either side of Meroë. Fields could be cultivated some distance away from the Nile itself, and sorghum and millet flourished. Cattle and other livestock could graze on the grasslands. There was also good hunting, because game was plentiful in the area.

Thus there were sound economic reasons for the Nubian move from Napata to Meroë. But the prime reason, historians suggest, was the availability of iron ore in the region. The craft of smelting iron had not yet been developed in Egypt. The Egyptians made tools and weapons of bronze and wood. They had had little reason to improve their tools because clearing land and plowing on the flat floodplains of the Nile were relatively easy. Moreover, there were few trees for wood for the charcoal fires necessary to smelt iron ore.

Like the Egyptians, the Nubians had experienced firsthand the superior iron weapons of the Assyrians. Now Meroë gave them the ideal opportunity to develop ironworking for themselves. They learned the secrets of the craft from the Assyrians and other western Asians who had first developed it. With iron hoes and axes, the Meroites could

This gold pectoral of the winged goddess Isis lay on the breast of a Kushite king buried at Nuri, near Napata, in the sixth century B.C. In Egyptian and Kushite belief, Isis was the mother of all pharaohs and the sister-wife of Osiris. Osiris had once been a king but had been murdered and hacked to pieces. Through her great love, Isis restored Osiris, who became ruler of the Underworld. Their son Horus ruled on earth as pharaoh. When each pharaoh died, he became "part" of Osiris and was reborn through a son who became the new pharaoh-Horus. Every pharaoh had a special Horus name, shown by a falcon glyph, and was a representative of the gods. ▼

plow and cultivate the earth and cut down trees. They could make better spears and arrows for hunting. Soon, Meroë had become a prime industrial center, producing so many iron implements that it has been nicknamed "Africa's Birmingham." To this day, giant mounds of ancient slag can still be seen near the town.

Thus, while Egypt and northern Nubia were entirely dependent on the Nile River and its fertile valley, the region around Meroë lent itself to the development of a more stable, mixed economy. Although life in Meroë still centered around the Nile, people no longer had to concentrate in towns and villages along the riverbanks. Most people were cattle herders and peasant farmers. They lived in mud and reed houses, clustered in small rural villages ruled by a head man or chief. They were seminomadic, moving their cattle between seasonal pastures. The king, the government officials, and the professional craftspeople lived in towns, the chief town being Meroë.

The king was an absolute monarch, just as he was in Egypt. But it seems that the Meroites enjoyed greater political freedom than the people of ancient Egypt.

The selection of a king required the consent of nobles and priests, and an unpopular king could be removed. The king's mother, or queen mother, was held in very high esteem, as she is in many other African cultures. The king probably received taxes in the form of tribute, whereas Egyptian taxes were assessed in advance according to the size and capacity of a person's fields. The king's wealth came from this tribute and from his personal control of trade.

Meroë was ideally located for the development of international trade. Just north of the Fifth Cataract, traders could cut across the desert to rejoin the Nile above the Second Cataract, thus avoiding the treacherous stretches of the river in between. From there, they traveled down the Nile to the market cities of Egypt. The Nile also took them southward, to the borders of present-day Uganda. Several routes extended east to the Red Sea, where the Romans had built ports to encourage trade. Meroë thus exchanged goods with peoples of the Mediterranean, southern Arabia, the Middle East, the East African coast, India, and perhaps even China. Merchants from these lands must have visited Meroë and perhaps traveled

even farther west, to Lake Chad and regions of West Africa. Iron hunting weapons and tools for mining and farming helped the Meroites to provide trade goods such as ivory, leopard skins, ostrich feathers, gold, and ebony. They also supplied iron implements for sale in distant markets.

The influence of the different cultures with which the Kushites had contact is seen in artifacts, reliefs, and buildings found at Meroë. As Egypt was overcome first by the Assyrians and then by the Persians (525 B.C.), the Greeks (332 B.C.), and the Romans (30 B.C.), these foreign influences were also felt far to the south, in the land of the Kushites.

Until very recently the cultural life of Meroë had been barely studied. The Kushite culture was thought of as merely a less sophisticated form of Egyptian culture, and for the first centuries after the move from Napata to Meroë, this was true. The Nubians had become so Egyptianized that their monuments and temples, their reliefs and inscriptions, all closely resembled those of ancient Egypt,

even though the people depicted were clearly Negroid and not Egyptian. The early rulers of Meroë even called themselves Lords of the Two Lands for centuries after they had ceased to rule in Egypt.

Over time, however, Meroë began to develop its own culture, entirely distinct from that of ancient Egypt. Various inscriptions show a gradual decrease in the use of the Egyptian language until it was finally replaced by a local language, known as Meroitic. Egyptian hieroglyphics were adapted to this language, and a new script was developed. Unfortunately no one has yet been able to decipher the Meroitic inscriptions, and their secrets— which could reveal much about Meroë's history—remain hidden.

The Meroites worshiped much the same gods as the Egyptians, including Amun. Just as in Egypt, priests were rich and powerful. Like Egyptian kings, who had to visit the temple of Amun at Thebes, the Kushite kings of Meroë had to undertake a ritual journey to

By 1909, linguists had proven that Meroitic was an alphabetic script with 23 letters. It is unrelated to any of the Nubian tongues spoken along the Nile, and does not resemble any other known language. Scholars hope someday to discover a text inscribed in Meroitic and another known language, such as Greek or Latin. This would enable specialists to "crack the code."

◄ During the first millennium, first the Greeks and then the Romans conquered Egypt. Their influence penetrated far into southern Nubia. This building, known as the Kiosk and used for royal ceremonies, is located on a trade route from the town of Naga in Upper Nubia to the Red Sea. It shows elements of Greek and Roman architecture.

the great temple of Jebel Barkal at Napata to be received and approved there by the gods. But beginning with the reign of King Nastasen from 328 to 308 B.C., the Meroites increasingly moved toward their own unique forms of culture and worship.

In Egypt, the ram was celebrated for its fertility, and Amun himself was often represented as a ram. By 225 B.C., when Ergamenes (er gah MEN ez) came to the throne of Meroë, the Egyptian ram god had been replaced with the Meroitic lion god, Apedemek (ah pe DE mek). He is often shown in reliefs as a man or snake with a lion's head. Sometimes, he has three faces and four arms.

A favorite subject in Meroitic engravings and sculpture is African animals, such as ostriches,

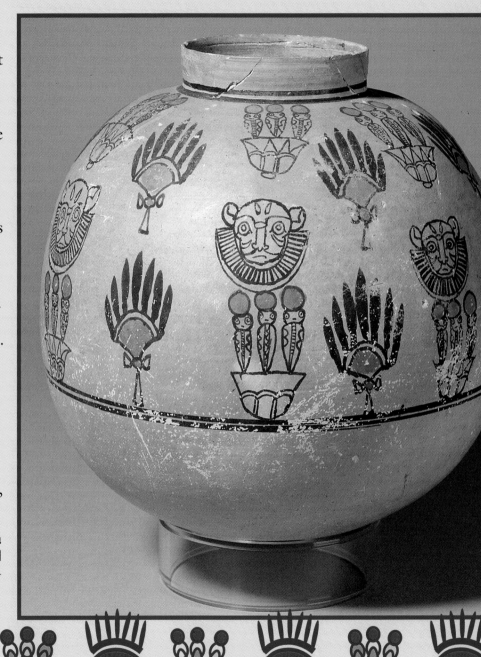

This pot was found with many others in a tomb at Faras, near Meroë. The lion head represents the lion god, Apedemek. ▶

giraffes, lions, and elephants. Living lions may have been kept at one temple to represent Apedemek, and elephants were used in war and for ceremonial purposes. In fact, the African elephants that the Romans used in warfare were almost certainly trained in Meroë, and knowledge of elephant training there may have come from India.

The Meroites excelled in making pottery, which has been found in great quantities at grave sites and in temples and is considered among the finest of the ancient world. This pottery reflects both the Mediterranean and the African traditions of Meroitic culture. Men made wheel-turned pottery that was similar to that made in Egypt. The styles of this pottery changed frequently as foreign influences came and went. Women, however, crafted handmade pottery that was truly African in its sources. Its style changed very little over the centuries, and similar wares are still made today in the Sudan and other parts of Africa.

For some time, Meroitic jewelry also resembled its Egyptian models. Most of this jewelry has been found in the

▲ Gold earrings from a pyramid tomb at Meroë show the head of the goddess Hathor, who was represented as having the ears or the horns of a cow. Hathor was believed to be the divine mother of all pharaohs.

graves of queens, who wore magnificent gold earrings, collars, amulets, and many bracelets and rings set with carnelians and other semiprecious stones. Rich and varied beads made of gold, silver, beryl, amethyst, and quartz have also been found. Disc-shaped ostrich egg shell beads were common then, as they are in the Sudan today. Flies, cowrie shells, and rams' heads were common motifs, as were engravings of Egyptian and even Greek gods and magic symbols.

Although itself much influenced by other cultures, Meroë undoubtedly had an impact on other parts of the African continent. It is possible that the knowledge of ironworking, for example, spread from Meroë into Central and East Africa. In these regions, better farming tools, especially the hoe, allowed people to produce more food, enabling the land to support larger populations. In other regions, better weapons led to the establishment of a central authority, such as a king or a governor, to organize an army and control the use of weapons. The great kingdoms of the western Sudan, such as Ghana and Mali, certainly relied on iron weapons to maintain their superiority over their neighbors, and they may have borrowed their ideas of statehood and kingship from Meroë.

The extent of Meroë's influence on the continent is still to be determined. For now, historians agree that Meroë was one of the most important cities in Africa, and that the Kushite civilization of Meroë was perhaps the greatest Africa has ever known.

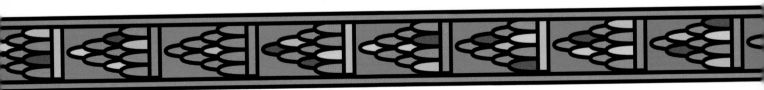

Aksum—The Christian Kingdom

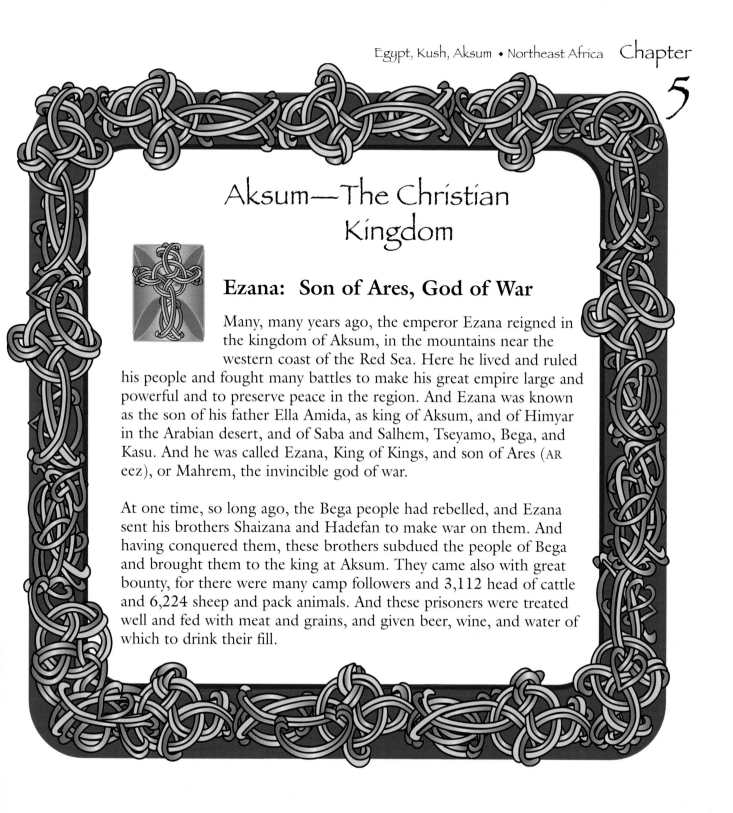

Ezana: Son of Ares, God of War

Many, many years ago, the emperor Ezana reigned in the kingdom of Aksum, in the mountains near the western coast of the Red Sea. Here he lived and ruled his people and fought many battles to make his great empire large and powerful and to preserve peace in the region. And Ezana was known as the son of his father Ella Amida, as king of Aksum, and of Himyar in the Arabian desert, and of Saba and Salhem, Tseyamo, Bega, and Kasu. And he was called Ezana, King of Kings, and son of Ares (AR eez), or Mahrem, the invincible god of war.

At one time, so long ago, the Bega people had rebelled, and Ezana sent his brothers Shaizana and Hadefan to make war on them. And having conquered them, these brothers subdued the people of Bega and brought them to the king at Aksum. They came also with great bounty, for there were many camp followers and 3,112 head of cattle and 6,224 sheep and pack animals. And these prisoners were treated well and fed with meat and grains, and given beer, wine, and water of which to drink their fill.

To Ezana came also in this multitude six tributary kings with their people, in number over 4,000. Their journey took four long months, yet Ezana sent to them each day 22,000 pieces of bread, and wine. When these people at last arrived before King Ezana at Aksum, he did not imprison them but set them free, giving them all kinds of food and clothing and allowing them to depart. Thence they went in peace and settled in a district called Matlia that belonged to the realm of Aksum. And to these kings, Ezana gave 25,141 head of cattle, that they might not hunger.

For his good deeds, Ezana wished the favor of his great father, the god Ares, and set up for him one statue of solid gold, one in silver, and three in bronze.

Now Ezana wished to rule in peace, but his kingdom was surrounded by warring peoples. After the people of Afan had killed and robbed all the merchants of a passing caravan of Aksum, Ezana made war on them. First, the king sent his armies, procured from his many provinces. Then the king himself followed and encamped at the place where the troops were assembled, and from there the soldiers set forth. And they killed and made prisoners, and a slaughter took place of the people of Afan, in all 705 men and women. And camp followers were taken prisoner, and as booty were carried off 31,957 cattle and 827 baggage animals.

Then the king returned in safety, together with his people, and he set up a throne in this region and committed himself to the protection of its people. And he let it be known that if any person or race would attempt to overthrow him, they would be conquered and removed and be rooted out of their country. And when this was done, Ezana offered 100 head of cattle and 50 prisoners as an offering of thanks to the great god of war, Ares, or Mahrem, who had begotten him.

Now, at this time, there lived in Aksum a Christian named Frumentius. He came from the Phoenecian (fuh NEE shun) town of Tyre and had lived in Aksum since he

was a child, for his father, visiting by ship, had been slain, and his ship captured. The boy Frumentius and his younger brother, who had traveled with their father, were left to live or die, but they were preserved by the mercy of the people and presented to the king. This king was Ella Amida, father of the child Ezana.

Ella Amida took in these children, Frumentius and his brother. There they lived, and the king observed that the younger brother was loyal, yet simple of mind but that Frumentius was wise and prudent, and at length, the king made him his treasurer and secretary. The king died soon after. His queen besought Frumentius, now a young man, to share with her the cares of government until her own infant son, Ezana, could command the throne.

Now Frumentius aided the queen in her government. At the same time, he sought out those Roman merchants who came down the Red Sea in their ships and who were Christians. And he bade them establish small chapels in convenient places to which they might repair for prayer. He provided them with sites for buildings and with everything they needed, in every way promoting the growth of the seed of Christianity in the kingdom. And the people of Aksum came, and many of them became Christians.

When Ezana, the young heir to the throne, came of age, and the queen no longer needed Frumentius by her side, Frumentius journeyed to the great city of Alexandria, at the mouth of the Nile. There, he made known to the Christian patriarch all the good work accomplished by Christians in Aksum. The patriarch at once conferred with his counsel and consecrated the good Frumentius and appointed him bishop of Aksum. They bade him return in the grace of God from whence he had come.

Frumentius returned to Aksum and was henceforth known as Abba Salama, the "father of peace." And in the year 327 A.D., Ezana, who was now king, renounced

his pagan beliefs and was baptized and became a Christian. From then on, he waged his wars under the banner of the Lord of Heaven and commanded that his followers, too, should be Christian.

By the might of the Lord of Heaven, Ezana made war on the Noba, to the northwest, for they had rebelled. They boasted that the king of Aksum would not dare to cross the Takkaze (tuh KAHZ ay), or Atbara, River. Two or three times they had broken their solemn oaths and killed their neighbors mercilessly. They had stripped bare and stolen the property of the king's envoys and messengers, whom he had sent to inquire into these thefts, and had stolen from them their weapons of defense.

Ezana had sent warnings to the Noba, but they had not heeded him and refused to cease their evil deeds. They heaped insults upon the king and then took to flight, and thus he made war on them. Ezana, King of Kings, rose up in the might of the Lord, and he fought them at a ford on the Takkaze. Thereupon they took to flight and would not make a stand. Ezana followed the fugitives for 23 days, killing and taking prisoners and capturing booty wherever he stopped. He burnt their towns, those built of bricks and those of reed, and his soldiers carried off their food, as well as their copper, iron, and brass. The soldiers destroyed the statues in the Noba's temples, as well as their granaries and their cotton bushes, casting them into the Nile. And the soldiers sank their ships, crowded with people, men and women, in the river.

Ezana set up a throne in that country at the place where the Nile and the Takkaze join. And the things which the Lord of Heaven had given him were men and women captives in many hundreds and cattle in number over 10,000 and 52,050 sheep. And King Ezana set up great stones in Aksum, on which were recorded the tales of his victorious deeds. And he begged the Lord of Heaven to make his kingdom strong and to conquer his enemies and to preserve his throne. Ezana, King of Kings, swore to rule his people in righteousness and justice. And for this he is known through all time.

The Aksumite Empire

The story of Ezana's conquests is partly taken from translations of his texts on three steles that he erected in Aksum sometime between A.D. 320 and 350. The information on his conversion to Christianity by Frumentius, the first bishop of Aksum, comes down to us from the scholar Job Ludolphus, writing in 1684. He in turn took his infor-mation from the Roman theologian Rufinus, writing in the fourth century A.D. Rufinus had the story "from the horse's mouth," namely, from Frumentius's own brother. Ezana's reign in the fourth century A.D. was a period of tremendous expansion in Aksum. Historians believe that the kingdom may at one time have included Kush, what

At its height, the kingdom of Aksum extended west to Meroë and east to Saba, in the Arabian desert. Trade routes connected Aksum and its port of Adulis with the rest of the known world. The exact location of other Red Sea ports that led to the growth of Meroë and Aksum is not known. ▼

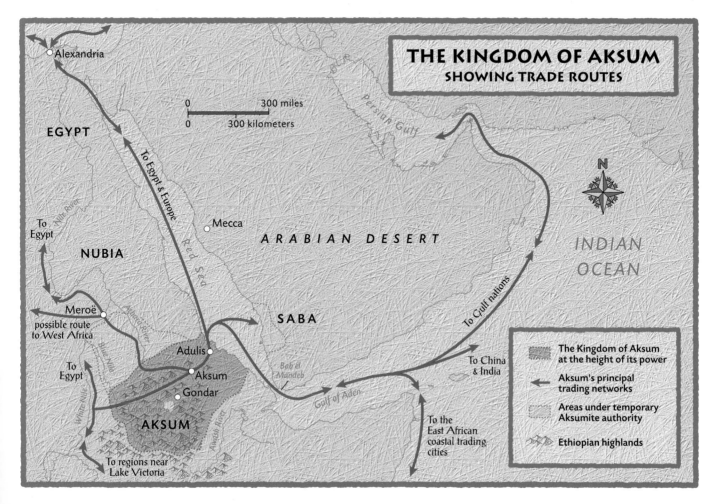

THE KINGDOM OF AKSUM
SHOWING TRADE ROUTES

0 — 300 miles
0 — 300 kilometers

Alexandria

EGYPT

To Egypt & Europe

Nile River

To Egypt

NUBIA

Mecca

Red Sea

Persian Gulf

A R A B I A N   D E S E R T

INDIAN OCEAN

N

Meroë
possible route to West Africa

Atbara River

Blue Nile

SABA

To Gulf nations

To Egypt

Adulis

Aksum

Gondar

White Nile

Awash River

AKSUM

Bab el Mandeb

Gulf of Aden

To China & India

To the East African coastal trading cities

To regions near Lake Victoria

The Kingdom of Aksum at the height of its power

Aksum's principal trading networks

Areas under temporary Aksumite authority

Ethiopian highlands

◀ In his inscriptions, Ezana first reveres the pagan war gods but later refers to the "Lord in Heaven"—the Christian God. Because of this reference, historians believe that Ezana was the first Christian king of Aksum. He may have converted in order to forge stronger trading links between Aksum and the Christian lands of the eastern Mediterranean. Perhaps influenced by the Greeks, Ezana had several types of coin minted, all bearing the Christian cross. During his reign, Christianity became the official religion of the kingdom. Since then, Ethiopia has maintained its own unique relationship with the Christian world. Today, age-old rituals, long lost in other Christian domains, are still practiced in Ethiopia.

In Egypt, Christianity split into two factions: the Monophysites and Diophysites. The Monophysites believed that Christ was a god and could not have been a human being as well. The Diophysites believed that Christ was both divine and mortal. Egyptian and Ethiopian Christians adapted to the Monophysite belief and formed the Coptic Church, so called after the ancient Egyptian, or Coptic, language. The Coptic language replaced Greek, which had been the traditional language of the Christian Church.

is now the southern Sudan, Aksum and its surrounding regions, and even parts of southern Arabia, across the Red Sea.

On the third of the three steles, Ezana boasts of having attacked and conquered the Noba, who occupied the region of Meroë. By this time, the great civilization of Meroë had declined almost to the point of nonexistence. Burials show that the royal line came to an end sometime in the fourth century A.D. The Meroitic language also seems to have "disappeared" around this time, perhaps because it was the language of the nobility, which had died out.

No one knows exactly why Meroë fell into decline. But historians have proposed several theories to explain the almost complete disappearance of one of Africa's greatest civilizations.

It is possible that the Noba—who may already have occupied the outlying regions of the "Island of Meroë"—attacked and conquered the Meroites before Ezana arrived. If this is true, Meroë would already have been weakened by the time of Ezana's arrival. It had lost a great deal of its trade, especially in ivory, through the growth of the Aksumite Red Sea ports. In addition, the Meroites had been cutting down trees to use as fuel in their iron-smelting forges for centuries. Eventually, supplies of wood must have run out, leading to a collapse of the iron industry. Since iron implements were a major item in exchange for goods from other regions, the end of ironworking would have led to a further significant loss of trade.

At the same time, historians suggest, the once-fertile area was probably overgrazed by huge herds of cattle, sheep, and goats. These factors led to the drying out and severe erosion of the savannah around Meroë. The environment that the Meroites had so cleverly chosen for their new capital almost 1,000 years earlier had been abused to the extent that it could no longer support the population. Ezana's attack on the Noba came as the final blow.

After the decline of Meroë, it faded from European memory for over 1,000 years. In 1768 the British explorer James Bruce traveled from Ethiopia down the Blue Nile into the Sudan, where he saw many ruins along a stretch of the Nile. Bruce guessed correctly that these ruins might be the remains of the ancient city of Meroë.

The Founding of Aksum

Ezana's steles were part of a centuries-long tradition in Ethiopia, according to which rulers inscribed their conquests (there are no records of defeats!) in stone. The tradition began with the Sabaeans (suh BEE unz), a Semitic people of Saba, in southwestern Arabia. The Sabaeans spoke and wrote a language related to that of the ancient Phoenicians, who inhabited what is now Lebanon. Like Phoenician, Sabaean script had no vowel sounds. They used their writing system to cut records of important events in stone. Some of these inscriptions were written and read from right to left. In others, alternate lines ran from right to left and from left to right.

The Ethiopians believe that the Sabaeans were the founders of the ancient Aksumite empire. This is confirmed in the tenth chapter of Genesis in the Bible, as well as in the writings of early Greek and Roman historians. It has also been confirmed by contemporary historians. At some time between the seventh and eighth centuries B.C., they say, the Sabaeans left their desert homelands and crossed the Red Sea in search of ivory for the Persian and Indian markets.

In the hills and fertile valleys of what is now northern Ethiopia, the Sabaeans found paradise. Rugged mountain ranges, some over 1,500 m (5,000 ft) high, protect the region from invaders. The mountains rise from the deserts of the narrow coastal plains and stretch west, where they give rise to the Atbara (Takkaze) River and the Blue Nile. In some places, two rainy seasons a year water the rich, red soil. To the southeast, the region is protected by a hostile desert barrier. And to the west, the mountains peter out into the grassy plains and desert wastes of southern Nubia.

In their desert highlands, the Sabaeans had already developed sophisticated techniques of irrigation and terracing. In their new home in Africa, widely differing geographical conditions created various miniclimates. Each region allowed a different type of agriculture, and the Sabaeans put their ancient skills

Ezana's steles were inscribed in the ancient Ethiopian languages of Sabaean and Ge'ez (ge EZ), and in ancient Greek. They depict Ezana as a conqueror but also as a man of compassion, who was kind to his prisoners. Of the hundreds of steles raised by different kings at Aksum, only this one remains upright. It stands over 30 m (90 ft) high, is flat on both sides, and is carved to represent a multistoried building. ▶

to good use. Wheat and barley could be grown, and sheep and cattle grazed on the lofty heights above 2,700 m (9,000 ft). Coffee, vines, and oilseeds thrived at 1,800 m (6,000 ft). In the hot lowlands, cotton, frankincense, myrrh, and aloes grew wild or were cultivated. Hundreds of species of useful plants and animals were native to this region, and the settlers hunted elephants for ivory, and ostriches for their plumes.

The Sabaeans left behind very few written texts dating to this period, but the archaeological remains clearly show their southern Arabian origins. At Yeha (YE hah), near Aksum, stands a remarkable tower—all that remains of a huge fortress, originally known as Awa (AH wah) and built in the south Arabian style. It is made of large stones, fitted together without mortar. Its walls are 1.5 m (5 ft) thick, and it stands 18 m (60 ft) high and 14 m (48 ft) wide. As in most places of antiquity, the architectural remains show us only how the rich and powerful lived, since they occupied the biggest and most durable buildings. Sabaean peasants and hunters appear to have lived in rectangular houses made of stone and mud.

Between about the third century B.C. and the first century A.D., the Sabaeans, who were farmers and traders, gradually mixed and intermarried with the local African population of farmers and pastoralist nomads. From this mix a new culture developed that bore little resemblance to the Sabaean culture. New styles of pottery and metalwork evolved during this period, along with a new language called Ge'ez . The Ge'ez language was related to Arabic and to the Semitic language Hebrew (the ancient language of the Jews), and also to the African language of the region. The Sabaeans, who were already literate, developed a script for it. Ge'ez is still used in Ethiopian churches and was the forerunner of Amharic, the main language spoken in Ethiopia today.

By the first century A.D., prosperous Ge'ez-speaking farmers and traders had established their capital at the inland location of Aksum. With its sheltered position in the mountains, its plentiful water supply, and its fertile land, Aksum was well chosen as the site of what was to become the capital of a great empire.

Ge'ez texts were first studied in Europe in the sixteenth century. Ethiopian scholars in Rome wrote the New Testament in Ge'ez in 1548. Ge'ez is closely related to Hebrew and Arabic.

ENGLISH	GE'EZ	HEBREW	ARABIC
house	bet	bayith	baitu

The earliest Sabaean settlers were quick to see the benefits of establishing trading settlements along the Ethiopian coast of the Red Sea. They were ideally located to profit from trade passing between Europe, Arabia, Asia, and eastern Africa. The earliest written report that we have of these harbors is the *Periplus of the Erythraean* (er IH three un) *Sea*, compiled in the first century A.D. Its author seems to have been a Greek ship merchant and mariner on his way from Egypt to the various Red Sea ports and perhaps farther, but his name remains unknown. Probably written in Greek, the original document is lost. A tenth-century copy of the account survives.

The Macedonian emperor Alexander the Great had conquered Egypt in 332 B.C. In 30 B.C. the Romans took over Egypt and ruled there for another 700 years. During these periods, Greek and Roman influence in Africa was strong, not only in Egypt but also in Nubia and, clearly, in Aksum as well. The author of the *Periplus* mentions that Aksum was at this time ruled by a king named Zoscales (ZOS kah leez), who was "upright and well versed in Greek literature." He must have been a very great king, for he is the only king the author of the *Periplus* mentions en route to India.

The "fair-sized village" of Adulis, on the Red Sea, is also mentioned in the *Periplus.* Clearly, Adulis had not yet become the thriving port that is indicated by the acres of ruins now lying under grass and sand where it once stood. From this early village, the author of the *Periplus* tells us, ivory was exported in great quantities. The ivory came from regions in the eastern Sudan and was transported via Aksum to the coast, along with highly valued tortoiseshell and rhinoceros horn.

All the major imports entering the kingdom of Aksum through Adulis are also listed in the *Periplus.* There was raw Egyptian cloth, as well as robes from the region near present-day Suez, colored cloaks, linen mantles, and many articles of flint glass, agate, and carnelian from Thebes. Brass

In Greek, *periplus* is the word for an account of a coastal voyage. The Greeks called the Persian Gulf, the Arabian Sea, and the eastern Indian Ocean the Erythraean Sea. The *Periplus* was written sometime in the late first century A.D.

"King Ellesbaas wore a linen skirt richly embroidered with gold and held by suspenders inlaid with pearls. His linen turban was also embroidered with gold and from it, four gold ribbons danced as the king shook his head. About his neck was a collar of gold and on his arms were heavy gold bracelets. He surveyed his court from a high, gold-encased, four-wheeled chariot pulled by a team of four elephants. Ellesbaas carried two small spears of gold and a gilded shield. His counselors stood nearby, carrying gilded spears and shields. The music of flutes dominated the court."
—*Description of the Ethiopian king Ellesbaas by the Roman ambassador to Aksum, sixth century A.D.*

for ornaments, soft copper for cooking utensils and jewelry, and iron for spears were all popular import items. Small axes and copper drinking cups also made their way from the farthest regions of the known world to Adulis. "For the king," the author of the *Periplus* further explains, were imported "gold and silver plate, made after the fashion of the country, military cloaks, and coats of skin. Likewise," the Periplus states, "from the district of Ariaca (ah ree AH-kah—northwestern India) across the sea were imported Indian iron and steel and Indian cotton cloth."

Six hundred years later, Cosmas Indicopleustes (ihn dih koh PLOY steez), a merchant from Alexandria, reported that ships from Aksum sailed to Ceylon, Persia, Arabia, India, and Byzantium. A Mesopotamian poet of the time wrote of an Aksumite sailing vessel: "Its prow cuts through the foam of the water just as a gambler divides the dust with his hand." These ships carried a wide range of valuable goods. Emeralds from the eastern Sudan were in great demand in India, Cosmas wrote, where they were sold "at a great price" and the proceeds invested in "wares of great value." Ivory and even living elephants were exported to the east, along with gold, spices, frankincense, and myrrh. From these distant regions, so Cosmas reports, the Aksumites returned with silk, cloves, and sandalwood.

Cosmas never refers by name to the kingdom of Aksum, but always to Aethiopia—the old Greek name for the region stretching from northern Nubia to the present-day Somali coast. However, he often refers to the city of Aksum as the capital of this region. By now, Adulis was a huge port, and Aksum itself, built on the profits of international trade, clearly wielded power far beyond its mountain ranges.

An Ethiopian woman sells finely made baskets in the modern Ethiopian town of Harar. ▼

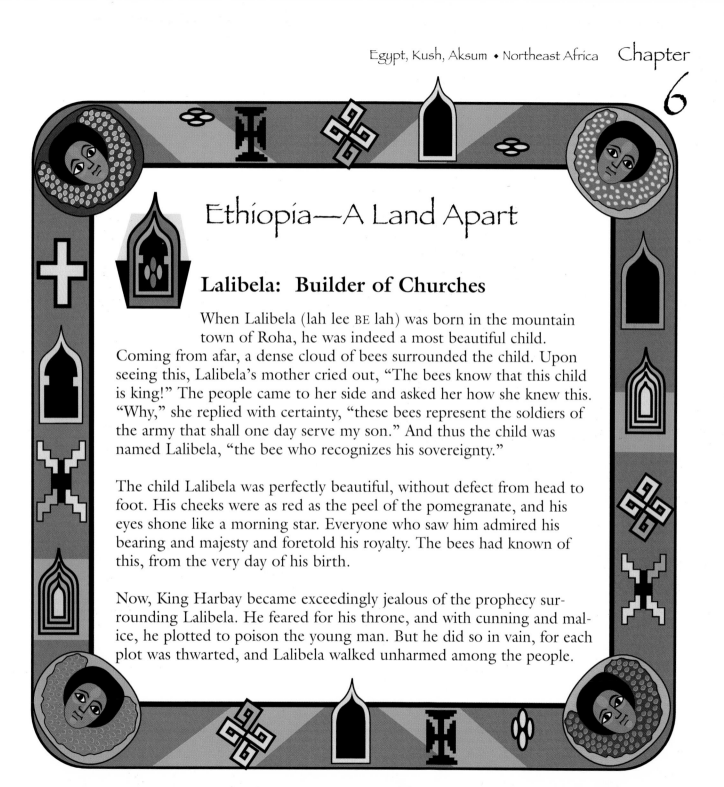

Ethiopia—A Land Apart

Lalibela: Builder of Churches

When Lalibela (lah lee BE lah) was born in the mountain town of Roha, he was indeed a most beautiful child. Coming from afar, a dense cloud of bees surrounded the child. Upon seeing this, Lalibela's mother cried out, "The bees know that this child is king!" The people came to her side and asked her how she knew this. "Why," she replied with certainty, "these bees represent the soldiers of the army that shall one day serve my son." And thus the child was named Lalibela, "the bee who recognizes his sovereignty."

The child Lalibela was perfectly beautiful, without defect from head to foot. His cheeks were as red as the peel of the pomegranate, and his eyes shone like a morning star. Everyone who saw him admired his bearing and majesty and foretold his royalty. The bees had known of this, from the very day of his birth.

Now, King Harbay became exceedingly jealous of the prophecy surrounding Lalibela. He feared for his throne, and with cunning and malice, he plotted to poison the young man. But he did so in vain, for each plot was thwarted, and Lalibela walked unharmed among the people.

As the young man grew older, it became apparent to all that he was indeed fit to be king. There came a time, then, when angels from heaven came to visit Lalibela. They transported him on high, to the first, second, and third heavens, where God showed him ten large churches, each built not of bricks and stones, but hewn from the living rock.

"It is not for the passing glory of this world that I will make you king," the Lord said, "but that you may construct churches like those you have seen here, in the heavenly realm."

At last, Lalibela knew his destiny, and he listened further as the Lord said, "It is for this purpose that I will give you the unction of kings and place you, the anointed one, over my people until you have built my sanctuaries."

At this, Lalibela descended in great glory to earth, where the Lord made himself visible to King Harbay. In fear and trembling, the king heard the Lord's words, who commanded him to abdicate his throne at once in favor of Lalibela, who would henceforth be king. And this was done, and Lalibela ascended the throne.

Thereupon, the Lord again spoke to Lalibela, saying, "The time has come to build churches like those I showed you in heaven. Arm yourself with the courage and strength necessary to accomplish this great work. Make haste, for many souls will be saved in these churches!" Lalibela wished to please the Lord, but he knew not how he was to begin this task. "Fear not!" said the Lord. "My angels shall descend from heaven to give you aid, that these churches may be built."

Thus fortified by the Holy Spirit, Lalibela first ordered the construction of many iron tools—some to cut the stone, others to hew it—and all implements necessary to fashion a church from the living rock. Then he sent messengers to Jerusalem and Alexandria, asking for men to help build the churches. And many hundreds of these men arrived, each eager to work on the houses of the Lord. From that

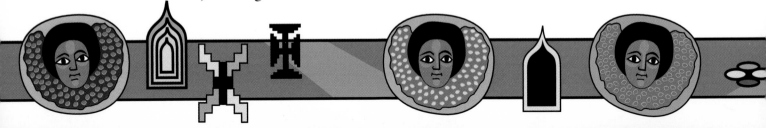

moment on, Lalibela no longer thought of his own needs, nor did he heed his wife, but he dreamt only and always of fulfilling his promise to the Lord.

When the tools necessary for this work were ready, Lalibela ordered all the workers to assemble before him. "Let every stonemason and excavator of the soil speak up," he said, "and tell me the wages he desires for this work that God has ordered me to complete. Speak up, and what you ask of me, I shall give, so that you do not say that I made you work against your will. I do not wish your work to go without reward, nor do I wish you to spread ugly rumors."

Each person thereupon made known his wages, and the king paid what he had promised to everyone, to those who cut the stone, to those who fashioned it, and to those who carried away the debris. He did this without fail from the day the work began until the day it ended.

The angels now visited Lalibela once more and gave him the dimensions of all the churches, both large and small. Lalibela chose the land upon which they would be built, and purchased it with gold. This was a great kindness on his part, because as the king he could have taken the land with one command.

Lalibela first built a church resembling the one that God had shown him. His men took their tools and dug deep into the rock, inch by inch, until the outer walls were carved from the stone. Then they descended into the deep ditch they had dug and carved their entrance from the granite. Day after day, year after year, they worked, cutting from the rock the nave and the aisles, and three chapels, each with its altar.

Lalibela embellished the inside and outside with paintings of the Holy Scriptures, that the people might know the ancient stories of the Virgin Mary and the saints. Into the rock, his craftsmen carved the beasts of the world and the two-headed eagle. They cut latticed windows in the shape of the cross, that light might enter the edifice.

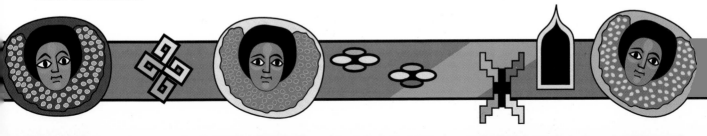

When the church was built, Lalibela named it Beta Maryam (BE tah MAH ree am), the House of Mary. Next to Beta Maryam, he built four other churches, all cut from the same rock, and named Debra Sina (Mount of Sinai), Golgotha, Beta Masqal (House of the Cross), and Beta Danagel (House of the Virgins).

Near to these five churches, Lalibela built another five, each one different in design, yet each conforming to the commands of the angels and to the wishes of God. Each church was the mirror of one in heaven, and each was the work of both angels and mortals, for angels came to help Lalibela and worked alongside the quarrymen and the stonemasons. The angels, more powerful than mortals, worked by day and by night, and in the mornings, the men marveled to see that their work of the day before had been tripled. They could not see the angels and therefore did not believe in them; but Lalibela saw and believed.

For 24 years, men labored on these churches of God. And when they were done, Lalibela, great king that he was, took off his crown and gave all of his possessions to the Church. He would no longer rule as king, he declared, for he wished to remain for the rest of his life in the service of God. And when he died, his wife, a pious and loving woman, caused the workers to carve one more church from the rock in memory of her dear husband, and it was named Abba Libanos. And the town of Roha was named Lalibela, after the great king.

Thus stand the ten churches of Lalibela forever. And he who gazes upon them will marvel and will never gaze his fill, for no tongue can describe them. King Lalibela fulfilled the destiny that was prophesied, and lived forever in heaven, among the saints.

This church at Lalibela, known as Beta Ghiorghis, or the House of Saint George, stands over 12 m (40 ft) high and is carved out of solid rock. It is said that Saint George helped in its construction and that his horse's hoofprints can still be seen in the courtyard. ▶

Chronicles Tell the Story

King Lalibela ruled in Ethiopia some time between A.D. 1200 and 1250. The story of how Lalibela built the famous rock churches, which still stand today, is adapted from a chronicle written by a fifteenth-century scribe and translated into English by the British historian Richard Pankhurst in 1967.

Lalibela's chronicle is much embellished by fantasy and fable. There is no doubt, however, that the king did indeed build the extraordinary churches at Roha, or begin the process of their building, for the work probably took much longer than 24 years. At their completion, Lalibela abdicated the throne and became a monk until his death, when he was made a saint. Roha, the town where he was born, was renamed Lalibela in honor of the much-loved king.

The Ethiopian chronicles began officially with the reign of King Amda Seyon (AHM dah ZYE un), or Pillar of Zion, from 1314 to 1344. They were almost always ordered by a king expressly to perpetuate his memory and glorify his deeds. While early chronicles were written in the ancient language of Ge'ez, the twentieth-century records are written in Amharic and have been translated into many languages. The chronicles vary greatly in length, style, and content. Some were written by scribes during the kings' own lifetimes. Others, like the chronicle of Lalibela, were written much later. Although events in these documents are sometimes exaggerated or move into the realm of myth, the chronicles have provided historians with invaluable information about Ethiopia. They continue the tradition of Ethiopian literature that goes back to the ancient stone steles of Aksum.

Apart from the royal chronicles and the Bible, the most revered Ethiopian book is the *Kebra Nagast*, or "Glory of Kings." It was written in the fourteenth century and tells the story of the famous romance that occurred about 1000 B.C. between King Solomon of Israel and Makeda (mah KE dah), queen of Sheba, or Saba, once a south Arabian province of the kingdom of Aksum. Many versions and translations of this book exist in Ge'ez, Arabic, Hebrew, and the European languages.

The *Kebra Nagast* relates how Queen Makeda heard tales of the wonders of Jerusalem and the wisdom of its king, Solomon. She was so impressed by these reports that she decided to visit the great king herself. She hoped to acquire some of his wisdom, so that she might better rule her own country.

The Falashas are Ethiopian Jews of the Agaw people living in the region near lake Tana. They claim descent from the nobles who accompanied Menelik back to Ethiopia, and they have suffered much persecution from Ethiopian Christians. In the tenth century, an Agaw chieftainess named Gudit attacked Aksum, overthrew the last of the Aksumite kings, burned down the city, and killed the royal princes. In the famine of 1985, some 7,000 Falashas were airlifted to Israel, leaving only a few thousand in Ethiopia. This Falasha woman, wearing the Jewish Star of David, is a skilled potter. She makes clay figurines representing various figures in Jewish history.

Then follows one of the most famous love stories the world has known. Makeda traveled to Jerusalem in a caravan of 797 camels and donkeys "beyond number," all heavily laden with gifts for King Solomon. During her six-month stay in Jerusalem, Solomon treated her royally, providing her with, among other things, "eleven changes of garments daily." So impressed was she with him that she gave up her pagan worship of the stars, the sun, and the moon and converted to Judaism, the religion of Israel. Solomon was equally impressed with Makeda, "a woman of such splendid beauty," who had come to him "from the end of the earth."

Makeda returned to Aksum pregnant with Solomon's child. She promised Solomon that if the child was a boy, he would one day return to greet his father. Makeda did indeed give birth to a son, and when he was grown, she kept her vow to Solomon and sent her son to Jerusalem. The boy resembled his great father so closely that the farmers he met along the way mistook him for the king himself.

Solomon was overjoyed. With holy oil, he anointed the young man and renamed him Menelik (MEN e lihk), meaning "how handsome he is." He ordained that no one other than Menelik's male descendants might rule in Ethiopia. And he ordered his nobles and counselors to send their firstborn sons to accompany Menelik back to his homeland. According to the legend, these counselors stole the Holy Ark of the Covenant, which had been kept in safety in Jerusalem, and took it to Ethiopia.

There is little historical foundation for the story of Solomon and Makeda. Nor is there proof that the Holy Ark was ever brought to Ethiopia. Yet the story has had a profound effect on Ethiopians. They believe that they are a people chosen by God to guard the Ark of the Covenant—symbol of the foundations of Judaism. Moreover, for 700 years, the Ethiopian sovereigns have based their legitimacy on their direct descent from Solomon and Sheba. Haile Selassie (HYE lee suh LA see), who was overthrown in 1974, was the last emperor of the so-called Solomonid dynasty.

The Holy Ark of the Covenant was a rectangular box that contained the two tablets of the Ten Commandments, as well as a pot of manna, various holy relics, and written laws. It was a symbol of the divine presence leading the Jewish people. The Ark was lost when Jerusalem was destroyed by the Babylonians in 587 B.C.

His Imperial Majesty Emperor Haile Selassie I died in 1975. He was the last of the Ethiopian Solomonid emperors. ▶

The Zagwe Dynasty

Lalibela belonged to a line of kings known as the Zagwe (ZAH gwe) dynasty, who took over the throne from the Aksumite kings in 1137.

Five hundred years earlier, Aksum had already declined in power. For centuries, the fragile resources of the region had been intensely exploited. Serious deforestation had taken place, and soil erosion had set in, leading people to abandon the area. In addition, the Aksumites were driven from their territories in the Arabian Peninsula by their rivals in trade, the Persians.

At the same time, the driving forces of Islam were sweeping across Egypt, Nubia, and North Africa. Although they did not conquer Ethiopia, the Muslims siphoned off most of Aksum's trade, redirecting it from the Red Sea through their own ports in the Persian Gulf. This led to the decline of Aksum's port, Adulis, and thus of the capital city itself. By A.D. 800, Ethiopia was an isolated Christian outpost, surrounded by hostile Muslim and pagan territories.

During the ninth century, the capital of the Aksumite kingdom was moved south, far from Muslim outposts, into the central highland region of Ethiopia. Cut off from the Christian communities in Egypt and the Middle East, the Ethiopians here developed their own, more African, Christian culture. Trade declined, and for 300 years the much-reduced kingdom, lost in its highland splendor, seemed to mark time. But when the founder of the Zagwe dynasty seized the throne, he established the capital of the kingdom at Adefa (ah DE fah), in the central highlands, and began a tradition of aggressive Christian expansion in all directions. Conquered territories were allotted Christian governors, and Christian missionaries set up monasteries on land granted by the king. These monasteries continued the ancient Aksumite traditions in art and architecture.

By the early thirteenth century, when Lalibela came to the throne, the Ethiopian kingdom had recovered from the fall of Aksum. There was renewed trade with Egypt, particularly in gold. A major export appears to have been women captured in wars with pagan peoples to the south. They were sold to wealthy Muslims as servants and concubines. The old connection between Ethiopia and the Christian diocese of Alexandria, in Egypt, was revitalized,

and Ethiopians made regular pilgrimages to the holy city of Jerusalem.

In 1270 the Zagwe dynasty was overthrown by the Solomonid line of kings, claiming descent from Solomon and Makeda, through the rulers of ancient Aksum. These kings ushered in a new era in Ethiopia. While they still visited the city of Aksum for coronation ceremonies, the Solomonid kings no longer maintained a palace and a capital city. Instead, the royal court moved around the country several times a year in tented camps.

This system enabled the king to keep in close touch with his subjects and to ensure that they paid their tribute. But so many people moved with the royal court that fuel and food supplies soon ran out wherever they camped. One report notes that these campsites could not be resettled for nearly ten years!

Despite this unusual system of mobile rule, the thirteenth to sixteenth centuries were ones of great splendor and wealth in Ethiopia. While trade was still important, tribute was the main source of income for the kings. Ivory, gold, slaves, livestock, and foodstuffs came pouring in to the royal camp. The camp was no rude affair, but a vast moving city of tents. There were sectors for the king and his family, for church officials, nobles, cooks, pages, artisans, and workers who accompanied the court. Tents housed the royal vestments and furniture, the bakery and kitchens, the justice court, and the prisons. When the court moved, it was in regal procession. The king, hidden from sight by red curtains, rode a mule, followed by the royal lions on chains. Two hundred men carried bread and meat, followed by the clergy in their glorious church robes, and thousands of followers.

With tribute coming in from all corners of the vast realm, the Solomonid kings and queens were able to patronize the authors of many literary works, for which the poetic language of Ge'ez was particularly well suited. Over five centuries, thousands of books and manuscripts were commissioned. The lives of saints and apostles and of Christ and the Virgin Mary were popular, along with less religious stories about Saint George and the Dragon, Alexander the Great, and other notable figures in

The Ethiopians raided the regions southwest of Lake Tana for slaves. It has been estimated that during the reign of Sarsa Dengel (1562–1597) about 10,000 captives a year were sold into slavery in Egypt and western Asia.

◀ Young deacons of the Ethiopian Orthodox Church wear gold filigree crowns and heavily embroidered capes to celebrate Christmas, or Genna, on January 7. Each church has its own crosses, like the one carried here. The crosses are usually made of brass or bronze and have been manufactured at Lalibela since the thirteenth century.

▲ In this seventeenth-century illustration to a text in Ge'ez, Christ rides into Jerusalem on Palm Sunday. Giacome Baretti, an Italian visiting Ethiopia in 1655, counted more than 10,000 manuscripts in the royal library. The Ethiopians believed that these were the oldest written works in the world, written by sages during the time of Moses. Baretti reported that 23 copyists worked full-time to transcribe deteriorating texts. The skins of 100 to 150 goats were needed to prepare the parchment for large manuscripts.

history. Along with this outburst of literature, Ethiopian art and music also flourished.

During this period, any possible rivals to the throne, along with their entire families, were simply imprisoned in a great mountain fortress. Yet neither mountains nor fortresses could protect Ethiopia from the winds of change that soon blew from far horizons.

ወሶቢ.ሃ፡በጸ.ሐ፡ኅቢ.

Epilogue

 While Ethiopia lived on in its medieval splendor, both Egypt and Nubia had lost all resemblance to their former glory. Egypt in particular had always been seen by its enemies as a crucial pivot upon which world trade turned. It was a breadbasket that could provide food for the desert peoples to the east and west and the Mediterranean regions to the north. It was the vital link between the markets of Europe and the riches of Africa, and the connection between the western world and the east.

After the Kushite Dynasty in Egypt had come to an end in 593 B.C., the ancient kingdom became a prime target for foreign invasion.

First the Assyrians, and then the Persians and the Libyans, conquered Egypt, establishing their own dynasties there. In the fifth century B.C., the Egyptian pharaohs regained the throne for a brief period. But in 332 B.C., the Macedonian emperor Alexander defeated the last Egyptian pharaoh and established a Greek dynasty that ruled for 300 years. The Greek government imposed a cruel system of taxation on the Egyptian farmers, or *fellahin* (fel uh HEEN). Most of the *fellahin* were left on the edge of starvation.

The Greeks founded the city of Alexandria—a hub of trade in the ancient world—and built a fleet of over 4,000 ships to expand trade in all directions. They established ports all along the Red Sea, which led to the rise first of Meroë, and then of Aksum. Despite these positive developments, however, Greek influence gradually corroded away the ancient Egyptian civilization and language, which had continued largely unchanged for 3,000 years.

Meanwhile, the Romans had occupied North Africa to the west of Egypt. By 30 B.C. they had wrested Egypt from the Greeks and proceeded to exploit the region even further for their own needs. To them, Egypt was nothing more than a supplier of grain for the vast Roman Empire. Roman rule was even more oppressive than the Greek system had been, and many Egyptian *fellahin* simply abandoned their farms and became bandits.

It was within this climate that Christianity, which had taken root in Palestine during the first century A.D. began to spread through Egypt, northeast Africa, and all of North Africa. To the oppressed Egyptians, the new religion offered hope of a better life after death. Alexandria became a center of Christianity where scholars studied Christian theology and the earliest bishoprics were founded. It was in Alexandria that Frumentius, first bishop of Ethiopia, was consecrated. Missionaries from Alexandria pushed south up the Nile into Nubia, which had become divided into three prosperous kingdoms after the fall of Meroë. By the sixth century, these kingdoms had become Christian, and the region soon became a refuge for Christians fleeing Roman persecution in Egypt.

Christianity remained a source of strength among the Ethiopian peoples, but this did not hold true in Egypt and Nubia, for in the city of Mecca, an "arm's length" away on the eastern shore of the Red Sea, the new religion of Islam, founded by Mohammed in the seventh century, was gathering momentum.

The pagan Arabians were immediately attracted to Islam. They were already familiar with the Jewish and Christian belief in one god. But Islam offered a less complicated alternative. Its laws were simple to follow. It was not ruled by a powerful upper class of priests, and it was easily accessible to everyone through the sacred book,

Much as the pharaohs did, the Egyptian government today requires farmers to provide food for the Egyptian population, as well as to cultivate cash crops such as cotton. The Egyptian *fellahin* raise corn, wheat, tomatoes, sugar cane, rice, oranges, potatoes, and wheat, as well as goats, sheep, and chickens.

Mohammed ibn Abdullah, a devout merchant of Mecca, longed for peace among the warring tribes of Arabia. Around A.D. 610, while in his 40s, Mohammed had a series of meditative visions. These revealed to him the One True God, Allah, as well as the rules and philosophy of a new belief system that Mohammed named Islam (ihs LAHM), meaning "submission." Muslims, who practice Islam, submit to the will of Allah. By A.D. 622 the codes of Islam had been written in the Qur'an, or Koran (kuh RAHN), the holy book of the Muslims. Mecca became Islam's holy city.

the Qur'an. Islam brought a common language—Arabic—and a new spirit of brotherhood to the war-torn clans of the Arabian desert. By the time of his death in A.D. 632, Mohammed had united thousands of Arabs in a formidable Muslim army. Though they had previously lacked the organization to conquer other lands, they now declared a holy war, or *jihad* (jih HAHD), against the rest of the world.

The Muslims swept northeast, conquering Mesopotamia and Syria. They raged to the northwest, bursting into the fertile Nile Delta. Ordinary Egyptians, who were fed up with Roman oppression, offered little resistance, and by A.D. 642 the Muslims had overthrown the Roman government in Egypt. At the point where the Nile spread into its delta tributaries, they established a new capital city called Cairo. From here, they could administer both Upper and Lower Egypt.

The Muslim rulers of Egypt allowed individual Egyptians three choices: Adults could pay a heavy annual tax; they could convert to Islam and avoid the tax; or they could die. Needless to say, most Egyptians—including many

Christians—chose to convert. Arabic was the official language of government and of the Qur'an, which all Muslims had to know by heart. Thus, the spoken language, literacy, and religion became inseparable. Arab traders penetrated Egypt's interior, bringing with them their language and their faith. Soon, Arabic had become the common language of the people, finally eclipsing the Coptic language, a descendant of ancient Egyptian.

Muslim rule was a great deal less oppressive than either Greek or Roman government. But Muslim unity did not last long. Conflict arose over who should succeed Islam's founder, Mohammed, and by the end of the seventh century A.D., Muslims had split into several factions. For 800 years, while the poor *fellahin* continued their age-old tasks of planting and irrigation, Muslim rivalries raged in the once-mighty kingdom of Egypt. As one dynasty replaced another, only to be replaced itself, the region was left wide open to yet another invasion—this time by the French emperor Napoleon, in 1798. Napoleon did not achieve his goal, which was to prevent British trade

▲ In the tenth century the Muslims built the great mosque of Al-Azhar in Cairo, where students studied Islamic religion and law. Today the mosque is one of the world's oldest universities, attended by students of Islam from many nations. This picture shows both men in modern dress and in traditional Muslim clothing. Today, almost 90 percent of Egypt's inhabitants are Muslims, and Egypt plays an increasingly important role in the Muslim world.

with the Middle East, but his invasion ushered the modern era into the ancient land of Egypt.

Egypt readily gave in to Islam. But the Christian kingdoms of Nubia confronted the mounted Muslim warriors with a huge army of archers. The Muslims retreated and negotiated a peaceful trade treaty instead. Ironically, good trade relationships helped spread Islam in Nubia, as nomadic Arab merchants traveled throughout the region. At the same time, where once the kingdom of Kush had flourished, the Funj of southern Nubia established their control. By the seventeenth century, they too had become Muslim.

Even the high mountain ranges of Solomonid Ethiopia were not immune from Muslim influence. During the tenth and eleventh centuries, Muslim merchants, com-

Mohammed Ali, an officer with an Ottoman army, helped to force Napoleon and the French out of Egypt in 1801 and took over the leadership of Egypt himself. Mohammed Ali welcomed European technology and modernization. He employed many European businessmen, army officers, and government officials and is regarded as the founder of modern Egypt.

Some 57 million people live in Egypt, and the population is growing rapidly. Most people live in the cities, where the majority must put up with crowded, run-down apartments, traffic congestion, and other typical city problems. ▼

peting with Ethiopians for ivory and slaves, set up trading settlements throughout the kingdom. By the fourteenth century, these had developed into Muslim states, which eventually grew to form the powerful kingdom of Adal (ah DAHL), between the Ethiopian highlands and the Red Sea. By 1526 a Muslim general known as Gran (grahn), "the left-handed," had taken over Adal and declared a *jihad* on Ethiopia. With unparalleled hatred of the Christian kingdom, Gran laid waste to the southern regions, burning churches, looting towns, and replacing Christian governors with Muslims.

At this point, Europe entered the fray. The Portuguese, who had established a mission in Ethiopia from 1520 to 1526, had just departed when Gran staged his attack. In despair the Ethiopian king begged the Portuguese for aid. In 1543 they sent a well-armed force led by Christopher da Gama—son of Vasco da Gama, the first European to sail around the Cape of Good Hope. Most of the Portuguese, including Da Gama, perished in battle, but not before they had killed Gran and seen his Muslim army disperse.

Still, peace did not come to Ethiopia, for the kingdom was now "invaded" by Oromo pastoralists from the south. The Oromo did not march as a conquering army. Instead, over time, clan after clan arrived, taking advantage of the south's weakened condition to claim new grazing grounds for their huge herds of cattle. The Ethiopian kings at the time paid little attention. They were focused on their northern territories and on the profitable slave trade with merchants on the Red Sea coast. By the early seventeenth century, it was too late for the kings to drive the Oromo out, for they had occupied the entire southern third of Ethiopia. The much-reduced kingdom established a fortress capital in the highlands at Gondar. But a century later, the Ethiopian kings had lost all power over the provinces.

From the eighteenth to the twentieth centuries, Egypt, Nubia, and Ethiopia became pawns in complex international power struggles over Africa. The British and French wanted to expand the ivory trade from the Sudan. The British also saw the Red Sea as a convenient shortcut to their colonial territories in India. Both nations invested

The great castle of Gondar was the center of the Ethiopian capital in the seventeenth century. ▶

Sudan is the largest country in Africa. The north is mainly desert, grassy plains form the central region, and tropical rain forests and swamps cover the southern region. There are more than 100 ethnic groups in the Sudan, among them the Nuba, Nuer, Dinka, and Kawahla. Over 100 languages are spoken. Most northerners are Arabic-speaking Muslims. Southerners practice indigenous religions. These differences cause frequent tension and fighting between the peoples of northern and southern Sudan.

vast sums of money in Egypt, building railroads and constructing the Suez Canal. Egypt had to borrow funds for these mammoth projects, and in 1876 the nation was forced to declare bankruptcy. To safeguard their own investments, the British army, with French agreement, occupied Egypt in 1882 and declared it a British protectorate in 1914.

A similar fate awaited Nubia. During the 1820s, Egyptian forces invaded Nubia, or the Sudan, as it was now called, raiding for ivory and slaves. They conquered the Funj and founded the city of Khartoum, where the Blue and White Niles converge. Sudanese hostility simmered until 1881, when a Sudanese holy man declared that he was the *Mahdi*—the "chosen one" who would revive the purity of the Muslim faith. The Mahdi's *jihad* raged with unabated fury across the Sudan, bringing most of the enormous region under his command. But in 1898, 20,000 Mahdist soldiers were mowed down

Devastating drought and famine have struck Ethiopia more than 40 times since the ninth century. In the tenth century, the Ethiopian king wrote to the patriarch at Alexandria, "All our men are dying of plague, and our beasts and cattle have perished, and God hath restrained the heavens so they cannot rain." In the famine of 1888–1892, more than two thirds of the population of Ethiopia died. In the 1970s and 1980s, millions of Ethiopians became homeless or starved to death.

by Anglo-Egyptian machine guns at the battle of Omduran. Just like Egypt, the Sudan was now, in effect, a British colony.

Alone among all African nations, Ethiopia managed to avoid European colonization. In the late 1800s, Menelik II became emperor. With all the shrewdness of the early Ethiopian kings, Menelik gained control of several former provinces and established a new capital city at Addis Ababa. He established diplomatic relations with the Europeans, introducing railroads, electricity, modern communications, hospitals, and schools to Ethiopia. In 1887 the Italians took over the northern province of Eritrea. But at the famous battle of Adwa in 1896, Menelik defeated the Italians' attempts to invade Ethiopia itself. In so doing, he saved the kingdom from European conquest.

In 1935 the Italians once again invaded Ethiopia. This time they attacked with bombs and poison gas and occupied the country for seven years. The Italians massacred over 700,000 Ethiopian citizens. They burned down 2,000 churches, destroyed 500,000 homes, and slaughtered millions of cattle, sheep, goats, and camels. In 1936, Emperor

◀ Thousands of people gathered for the opening of the Suez Canal in 1869. The first ship in the convoy carried Napoleon's wife, the empress Eugenie. The canal gave international shipping a shortcut between Europe and the Indian Ocean. It also enabled European shipping to dominate Egyptian trade.

Haile Selassie—last in the Solomonid line—appealed to the League of Nations for help, but his words fell on deaf ears. For seven years, Ethiopian patriots kept up relentless guerilla resistance. But it was only when the Italians invaded British-held Sudan in 1940 that the British reacted to Italian aggression in the northeast. African forces from all the British colonies in Africa were summoned to Ethiopia, and by May 1941 the British had liberated the kingdom from the Italians. Haile Selassie was reestablished on the throne in Addis Ababa and ruled until he was deposed by the military in 1974.

Today, Egypt, the Sudan, and Ethiopia are independent nations. Ancient ways of life persist in all three regions, and age-old internal ethnic, political, and religious differences have not been resolved. These, as well as disputes with neighboring countries, continue to be the source of frequent war and rebellion. Given the history and geography of the nations of northeastern Africa, this picture is not likely to change within the near future.

At the battle of Adwa in 1896, the army of the Ethiopian emperor Menelik II defeated the Italians, who had occupied Eritrea.▼

Pronunciation Key

Some words in this book may be new to you or difficult to pronounce. Those words have been spelled phonetically in parentheses. The syllable that receives stress in a word is shown in small capital letters. The following pronunciation key shows how letters are used to show different sounds.

a	after	(AF tur)	oh	flow	(floh)	ch	chicken	(CHIHK un)
ah	father	(FAH thur)	oi	boy	(boi)	g	game	(gaym)
ai	care	(kair)	oo	rule	(rool)	ing	coming	(KUM ing)
aw	dog	(dawg)	or	horse	(hors)	j	job	(jahb)
ay	paper	(PAY pur)				k	came	(kaym)
			ou	cow	(kou)	ng	long	(lawng)
e	letter	(LET ur)	yoo	few	(fyoo)	s	city	(SIH tee)
ee	eat	(eet)	u	taken	(TAY kun)	sh	ship	(shihp)
				matter	(MAT ur)	th	thin	(thihn)
ih	trip	(trihp)	uh	ago	(uh goh)	thh	feather	(FETHH ur)
eye	idea	(eye DEE uh)				y	yard	(yahrd)
y	hide	(hyd)				z	size	(syz)
ye	lie	(lye)				zh	division	(duh VIHZH un)

For Further Reading

(***** = recommended for younger readers)

Beckwith, C., and Angela Fisher. *African Ark*. New York: Harry N. Abrams, 1990.

Boyd, Herb. *African History for Beginners*. New York: Writers and Readers Publishing, 1991.*

Breasted, James H. *Ancient Records of Egypt*. New York: Russell & Russell, 1962.

Brooks, Lester. *Great Civilizations of Ancient Africa*. New York: Four Winds Press, 1971.*

Brunton, W., et al. *Kings and Queens of Ancient Egypt*. London: Hodder & Stroughton, 1924.

Budge, E. A. Wallis. *A History of Ethiopia, Nubia, and Abyssinia*. Oosterhout, The Netherlands: Anthropological Publications, 1966.

Clayton, Peter A. *Chronicle of the Pharaohs*. London: Thames and Hudson, 1994.*

Cottrell, Leonard. *Five Queens of Ancient Egypt*. New York: Bobbs-Merrill, 1969.

Davidson, Basil. *Africa in History*. New York: Macmillan, 1991.

——*African Kingdoms*. New York: Time-Life Books, 1966.

——*A Guide to African History*. New York: Doubleday, Zenith Books, 1965.

——*The Lost Cities of Africa*. Boston: Little, Brown, 1970.

Fage, J. D. and R. Oliver. *The Cambridge History of Africa*. New York: Cambridge University Press, 1978.

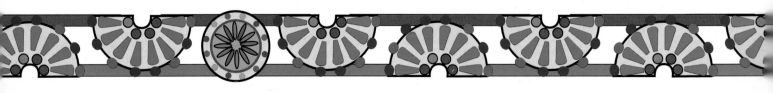

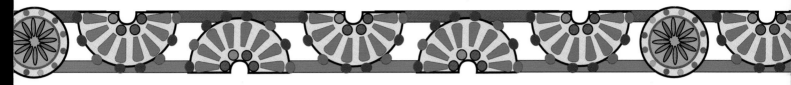

Jenkins, E. *A Glorious Past: Ancient Egypt, Ethiopia, and Nubia*. Philadelphia: Chelsea House, 1995.*

Johnson, E. Harper. *Piankhy, The Great*. New York: Thomas Nelson & Sons, 1965.*

Joseph, Joan. *Black African Empires*. Franklin Watts, 1974.*

Harris, Joseph E. *Africans and Their History*. New York: New American Library, 1987.

Hintze, Fritz, and Ursula Hintze. *Civilizations of the Old Sudan*. Leipzig: Edition Leipzig, 1968.

Hugon, Anne. *The Exploration of Africa from Cairo to the Cape*. New York: Harry N. Abrams, 1993.*

Jezman, C. *The Ethiopian Paradox*. London: Oxford University Press, 1963.

Ki-Zerbo, Joseph. *Die Geschichte Schwarz-Afrikas (The History of Black Africa)*. Wuppertal: Peter Hammer, 1979.

Kwamena-Poh, Michael. *African History in Maps*. London: Longman, 1982.

Mazrui, Ali. *The Africans—A Triple Heritage*. Boston: Little, Brown, 1986.

McEvedy, Collin. *The Penguin Atlas of African History*. London: Penguin Books, 1980.*

Murray, Jocelyn. *Cultural Atlas of Africa*. New York: Facts on File, 1989.*

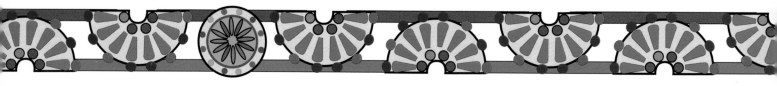

Oliver, Roland. *The African Experience*. New York: HarperCollins, 1991.

Oliver, Roland, and J. D. Fage. *A Short History of Africa*. 6th ed. London: Penguin Books, 1988.

Pankhurst, Richard K. P. *The Ethiopian Royal Chronicles*. London: Oxford University Press, 1967.

Pankhurst, Sylvia. *Ethiopia: A Cultural History*. Woodford Green: Lalibela House, 1959.

Perl, L. *History of East Africa*. New York: William Morrow, 1973.

Redford, Donald B. *History and Chronology of the Eighteenth Dynasty of Egypt*. Toronto: University of Toronto Press, 1967.

Ruffle, J. *The Egyptians*. Ithaca, N.Y.: Cornell University Press, 1977.

Save-Soderbergh, T. *Temples and Tombs of Ancient Nubia*. London: Thames and Hudson (UNESCO), 1987.

Shaw, Ian, and Paul Nicholson. *The Dictionary of Ancient Egypt*. New York: Harry N. Abrams, 1995.*

Shinnie, P. L. *Meroe, A Civilization of the Sudan*. New York: Frederick A. Praeger, 1967.

Stacey, Tom. *Peoples of the Earth*. Tom Stacey and Europa, 1972.*

Thompson, Elizabeth Bartlett. *Africa Past and Present*. Boston: Houghton Mifflin, 1966.

Vercoutter, Jean. *The Search for Ancient Egypt*. New York: Harry N. Abrams, 1992.*

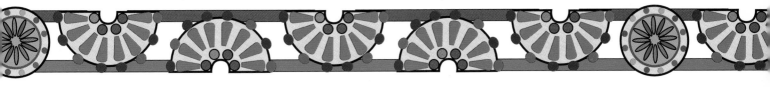

Index

Adal, 94
Addis Ababa, 97, 98
Adulis, 69, 75, 76, 85
Aethiopia, 46, 48, 76
agriculture, 10, 24–25
Ahmose, 13, 20, 21
Aksum, 11–12, 65–76, 82, 83, 85, 87, 90
Alexander the Great, 49, 74, 87, 89
Alexandria, 67, 78, 85, 89, 90
Amenirdis I, 40
Amun-Re (Amun), 13–17, 20, 33, 36, 40, 43, 56, 59, 62
Apedemek, 62, 63
archeological finds, 44, 48, 51, 52, 73
Ark of the Covenant, 84
Assyrians, 42, 43, 44, 56, 57, 59, 89
Aswan, 8, 17, 18, 40, 44, 46, 51
Aswan High Dam, 10, 11, 44

Baretti, Giacome, 88

Bekenrenef, 42
Bible, 42, 48, 72
Blue Nile, 7, 8, 71, 72
Breasted, James Henry, 19, 20, 33
British, 91, 94, 96, 97, 98
Bruce, James, 71

Cairo, 91
cartouche, 14
Champollion, Jean François, 14
Christianity, 12, 49, 67–68, 69, 70, 85, 90, 93, 94
churches (rock), 78–80, *81,* 82
Coptic Church, 70
Coptic language, 70, 91
Cosmas Indicopleustes, 75–76

da Gama, Christopher, 94
Deir el-Bahri, 15, 19, 28, *30,* 33
divine kingship, 21
dynasties, 23–25, 40, 41, 42, 43, 51, 84, 85, 89, 91

Egypt, 6–33, 39, 40, 42, 43, 44, 49, 51–53, 56, 57, 58, 59, 62, 74, 85, 89–90, 91, 93, 94, 96, 98
Ergamenes, 62
Ethiopia, 7, 11, 12, 40, 48, 70, 72, 77–88, 89, 90, 94, 97–98
Ezana, 12, 65–72

Falashes, 83
fellahin, 89, 90, 91
floods, 7, 10, 23, 25, 39, 42
French, 91, 93, 94, 96
Frumentius (Abba Salama), 66–67, 69, 90

Ge'ez language, 72, 74, 82, 87, 88
gods, 7, 8, 9, 13–15, 20, 21, 30–31, 42, 53, 57, 59, 62, 70
Gondar, 11, 94, *95*
Gran, 94

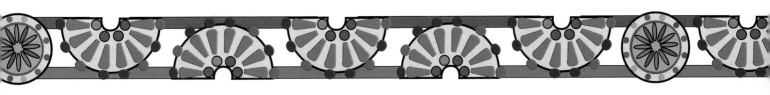

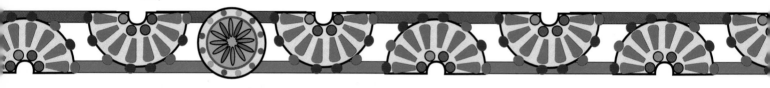

Greeks, 14, 23, 25, 44, 46, 48,
　　59, 61, 70, 72, 74,
　　89–90, 91

Hatshepsut, 9, 13–22, 24,
　　26–31
Herakleopolis, 35, 36, 38
Hermopolis, 35–38, 41
Herodotus, 6, 7, 46, 56
hieroglyphics, 8, 14, 19, 24, 53,
　　59

Intermediate Periods (Dark
　　Ages), 24, 25, 41, 52
ironworking, 56–58, 59, 64, 71
Islam, 85, 90–93
Italians, 97–98

Jebel Barkal, 11, 43, *45*, 56, 62
Jerusalem, 42, 78, 82–83, 84,
　　87
jewelry, 63–64
jihad, 91, 94, 96
Judaism, 83–84
ka, 13, 20, 21
Karnak, 17, 20, 30, 42

Kashta, 34, 40
Kawa, 43
Kebra Nagast, 82
Kerma, 51–52
Khnum, 13, 14, 21
Kush, 8, 11, 12, 18, 34–49,
　　53, 56, 71. *See also*
　　Nubia, Sudan.

Lalibela, 77–82, 85
Leontopolis, 41
Libya, 40, 49, 89
Lower Egypt, 8, 14, 15, 18,
　　25–26, 28, 35, 40,
　　42, 91
Lower Nubia, 8, 10, 48,
　　50, 51
Ludolphus, Job, 69

Mahdi, 96–97
Makeda, 82–84, 87
Manetho, 23, 24
Mecca, 90, 91
Memphis, 18, 26, 38–39, 40,
　　42, 43, 44
Memphite Theology, 42

Menelik, 83–84
Menelik II, 97, 98
Menes (Narmer), 21, 26, 28
Meroitic language, 59, 71
Meroë, 11, 18, 48, 50–64, 69,
　　71, 90
Middle Kingdom, 24, 25, 51
Mohammad Ali, 93
Mohammed ibn Abdullah, 90,
　　91
monuments, 10–12, 43, 73.
　　See also obelisks,
　　pyramids, tombs.
Muslims, 85, 91–94

Namlot, 35, 36–38, 41
Napata, 11, 18, 34, 40, 42, 43,
　　44, 48, 53, 56
Napoleon, 14, 91, 93
Nastasen, 62
Nefru-Re, 31
New Kingdom, 24, 25, 43
Nile River, 6–9, 21, 34, 50, 51,
　　52, 56, 58, 91
Noba, 48–49, 68, 71
nomes, 18

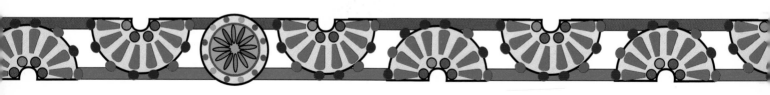

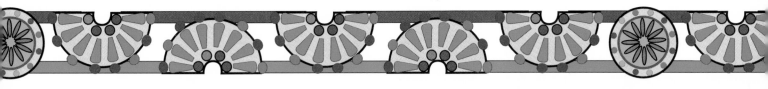

Nubia, 8, 11, 18, 20, 24, 40, 42, 44, 46, 48, 49, 50–53, 56–59, 72, 74, 85, 89, 90, 93, 94, 96. *See also* Kush, Sudan.
numbers, 9

obelisks, 8, 17–18, 20
Old Kingdom, 24, 25, 51
Oromo, 94
Osorkon III, 40

Pankhurst, Richard, 82
Papyrus Westcar, 20
Periplus of the Erythraean Sea, 74, 75
Persians, 59, 85, 89
pharaohs, 8, 9, 14, 20, 21, 22, 30, 49, 52, 57, 89
Piye, 11, 34–42, 53
Pliny, 46
Portuguese, 94
pottery, 63, 74
Prester John, 94
Punt, 15–17, 19
pyramids, 8, *46–47,* 53, 56

racial bias, 49
Rameses II, 10, 11, 24, 43, 53
Rameses III, 23
Re, 20
Reisner, George, 49
Roberts, David, 49
Romans, 14, 25, 40, 44, 46, 48, 49, 58, 59, 61, 63, 67, 69, 72, 74, 90, 91
Rosetta Stone, 14
Rufinus, 69

Sabaeans, 72–74
Schwaller, R. A., 9
Selassie, Haile, 84, 98
Senenmut, 17, 30, 31
Seyon, Amda (Pillar of Zion), 82
Shabaka, 42, 43
Siculus, Diodorus, 46
Solomon, 82–84, 87
Solomonid dynasty, 84, 87, 93, 98
Somalia, 48
Strabo, 46
Sudan, 8, 10, 48, 50, 63, 64, 71, 94, 96–97, 98

Suez Canal, 96–97

Taharka, 42–44
Tanis, 41, 43
Tanutamun, 44, 56
Tefnakht, 35–39, 41, 42
Thebes, 9, 17, 36, 40, 41, 42, 43, 44, 59, 75
Thoth, 7, 13
Thutmose I, 13, 15, 26, 28, 30, 33
Thutmose II, 26, 28
Thutmose III, 20, 23, 26, 28, 30–33, 52
tombs, 8, 9, 19, 20, 26, 28, 30, *46–47,* 49, 52
trade routes, 51, 58–59, 69, 74–76, 85, 89–90

Upper Egypt, 8, 14, 15, 18, 25–26, 28, 34, 35, 40, 91
Upper Nubia, 8, 48

Zagwe dynasty, 85, 87
Zoscales, 74–75

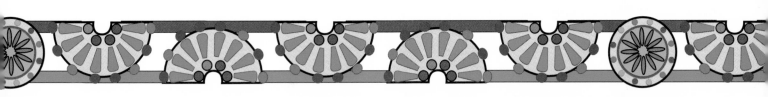

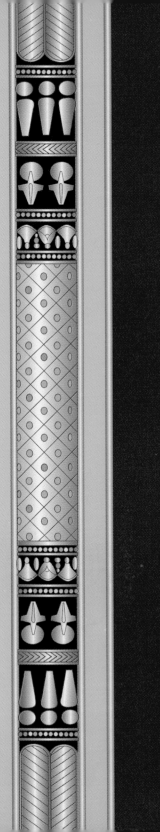